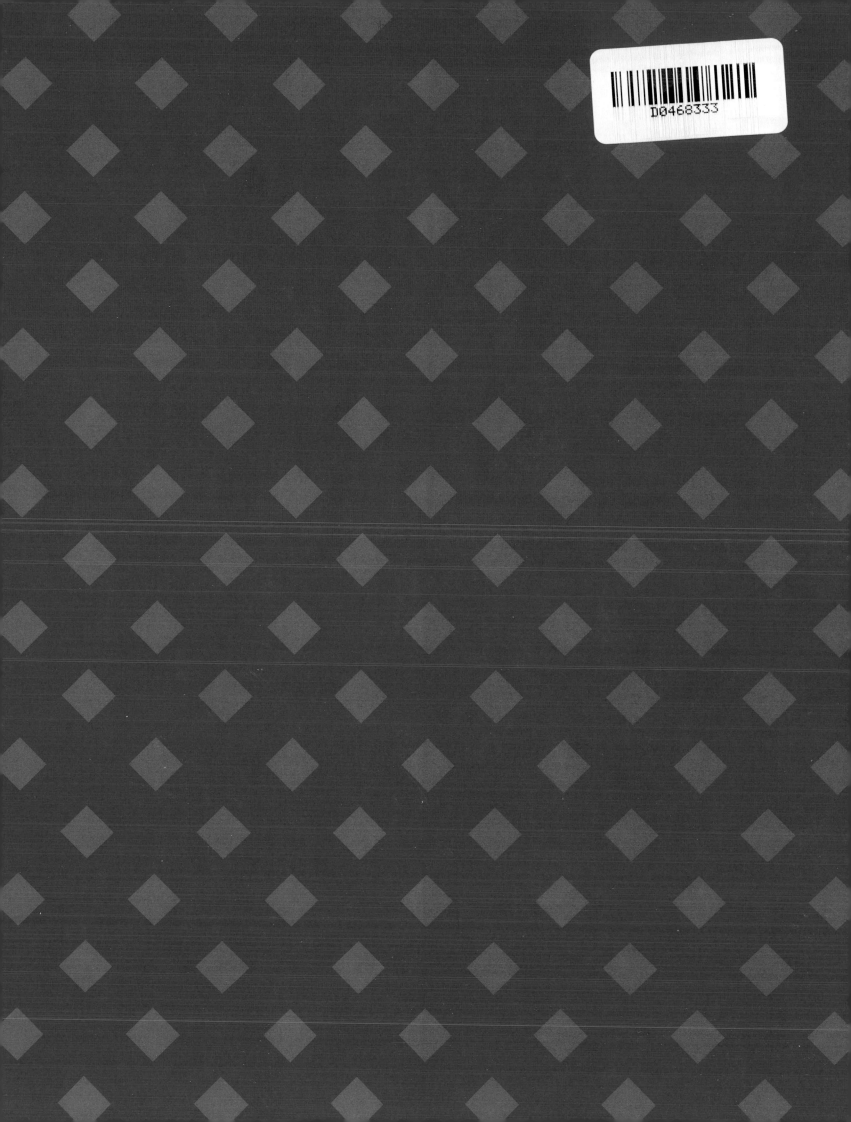

THE NEW GUIDE TO
NEEDLECRAFT
SKILLS AND TECHNIQUES

THE NEW GUIDE TO

NEEDLECRAFT

SKILLS AND TECHNIQUES

Lucinda Ganderton

Photographs by James Duncan

ULTIMATE
EDITIONS

For my sister, Emma, with love.

First published in 1996 by Ultimate Editions

© Anness Publishing Limited 1996

Ultimate Editions is an imprint of
Anness Publishing Limited
1 Boundary Row, London SE1 8HP

This edition distributed in Canada by Raincoast Books Distribution Limited

ISBN 1-86035-039-9

A CIP catalogue record for this book is available from the British Library.

Publisher: Joanna Lorenz
Senior Editor: Belinda Wilkinson
Designer: Martin Lovelock
Photographer: James Duncan
Step Photographer: Madeleine Brehaut
Stylist: Lucinda Ganderton

Thanks to Anne Cree

Printed in Singapore by Star Standard Industries Pte. Ltd.

1 3 5 7 9 10 8 6 4 2

Previously published as part of a larger compendium, *The Complete Guide to Needlecraft*.

Measurements
Both imperial and metric measurements have been given in the text.
Where conversions produced an awkward number, these have been rounded
for convenience, but will produce an accurate result if one system is followed throughout.

Contents

Embroidery

Embroidery can be defined as the decoration of an existing fabric with ornamental stitches. The art has a long and fascinating history, originating in the opulent colours and stitchery of the Middle East, which arrived in Europe during the time of the Roman Empire. Historically, splendid embroidery was an outward expression of wealth: gold or silver threads, the finest silks, pearls and precious stones have always been used to adorn the robes of kings and emperors and to symbolize their power. Hand-embroidered clothes still have great ceremonial significance: many brides wear gowns encrusted with beads and elaborate stitchery, and whitework christening gowns are treasured heirlooms. Much of the early work that has survived is ecclesiastical. Church embroidery was influenced by the rich ornament of Byzantium and reached its peak in the *Opus Anglicanum*, or English Work, of the thirteenth and fourteenth centuries. A trade network existed via which the London workshops sent vestments to the popes in Rome.

The majority of the secular embroidery work was of a military and heraldic nature, the most famous

A bag of oranges was the inspiration for this machine-embroidered piece, which is worked on paper over a watercolour illustration.

example being the Bayeux Tapestry. It dates from shortly after the invasion of England by William the Conqueror in 1066 and gives a narrative record of the events of that year.

Heraldic banners and flags were used in battle to identify groups of soldiers and are still carried ceremonially by the armed forces. Alongside the military versions, the old craft guilds and later, trade unions, developed pictorial banners, embroidered with their coats of arms. Members would march behind these as a symbol of solidarity.

Domestic embroidery flowered in the sixteenth century. Contemporary aristocratic portraits show elaborate dresses, often decorated with

blackwork. This was the period when embroidery ceased to be the sole preserve of the nobility, as it spread throughout Europe to the rising merchant classes.

Indigenous embroidery developed strong national characteristics. Different cultures specialized in different techniques, utilizing locally available materials. Exquisite floral Chinese embroidery used fine silk threads, while Native Americans incorporated stained porcupine quills and glass beads in their richly decorative work.

Patterns and techniques, however, have always travelled and developed. Geometric cross stitch, the most widely

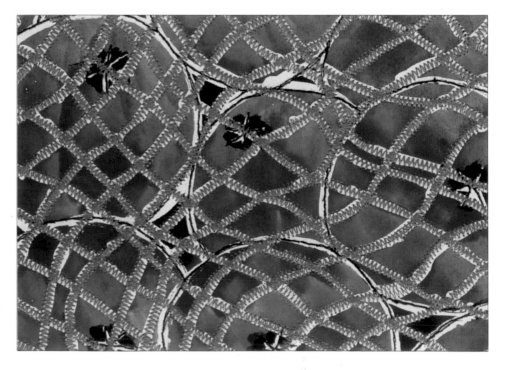

Right: This antique embroidered slipper – which was never made up – is worked on a black felt background in laid gold thread and silk floss.

Left: Cross stitch samplers were a learning exercise for the children who made them. Stylized birds, flowers and trees were worked alongside alphabets and improving mottoes.

In the nineteenth century the passion for interior decoration reached great heights. Wealth generated by developing industries meant that more and more people were moving into new homes and wanted to make them unique. By the 1870s most middle-class interiors were decorated with an astonishing array of embroidered piano covers, fire screens, pincushions, candle shades and bell pulls. The Art Needlework movement sought to encourage embroiderers to express themselves by experimenting with new materials and their ingenuity encompassed sewing with ribbons and bows, and on to painted silk.

Taste in the early twentieth century moved away from the excesses of the preceding years and towards a more refined style. Art Nouveau and Art Deco styles were both interpreted in embroidery, but the scope for new design and reworking of tradition has never been greater than it is today.

spread folk art technique in Europe, was taken to the New World by Pennsylvania Dutch immigrants. Settlers took with them their individual textile traditions, but life in America was different and hard, with cloth and thread in short supply. Needlework schools existed in New England from the early eighteenth century, and imported materials and fabrics were more generally available there than on the frontier but, even so, yarn was expensive. Tutors tended, therefore, to instruct embroiderers to outline designs, not to fill them in and, above all, to be economical with the precious thread.

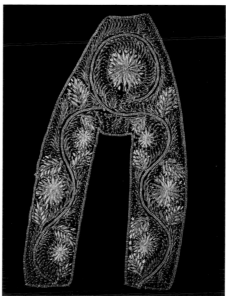

Right: Embroidery has always been used in conjunction with other needlecrafts: strong, simple stitches emphasize the shapes of this contemporary folk-art style appliqué.

Embroidery
Tools and Materials

An inspiring selection of fabrics and threads is available which, with imagination, can be combined to produce individual and exciting embroideries. The basic equipment needed is minimal: every sewing box should contain the tools listed, along with pins and sewing thread. A steam iron is necessary for all needlecrafts, to finish work professionally.

THREADS
Threads come in a broad spectrum of colours. Silk and metallic threads give texture, but the most popular threads are 6-stranded cottons which can be separated for fine stitching. Perlé cotton is a single thread with a shiny finish. Wool threads, including finely spun crewel yarn and 3-stranded Persian yarn, are used singly for embroidery. Machine threads can be glossy or metallic, and some are even space-dyed with stripes.

FABRIC
Ordinary linens are used for free stitchery but single-thread even-weave linens have a regular mesh so that the stitches are even. They are designed for counted thread and pulled or drawn work. There are several types of double-thread even-weaves. The finest is Hardanger fabric which has a count of 22, i.e., there are 22 threads to 2.5cm (1in). 14-count Aida cloth is suitable for cross stitch and 6-count Binca is ideal for beginners. Narrow bands of fabric with woven edges are also available.

FRAMES
Adjustable tapestry or scroll frames are best for large pieces, while hoops suit most other work. They can be bought with stands so that the user's hands are left free to work the piece. Round plastic frames with metal inner rings are especially good for machine embroidery.

TOOLS AND ACCESSORIES
Needles come in different widths and lengths, the most useful being large-eyed crewel needles. Tapestry needles are thick and blunt, while chenille needles are larger but pointed.

Long-bladed dressmaker's shears are essential for cutting fabric and a small pair of sharp embroidery scissors is needed for threads. An unpicker is always very useful for correcting mistakes and a thimble protects the finger.

Water-soluble or fading dressmaker's felt-tip pens are used to mark directly on to fabric. Carbon pencils and dressmaker's carbon will transfer designs from paper to cloth.

From top to bottom, three types of even-weave linen, and one non even-weave linen.

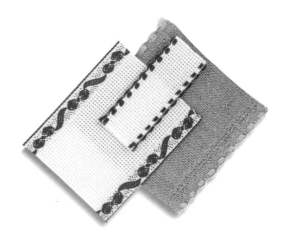

From left to right, woven Aida bands with decorative edging in blue and red, and natural linen.

From top to bottom, Hardanger fabric, Aida cloth in white and green, Binca.

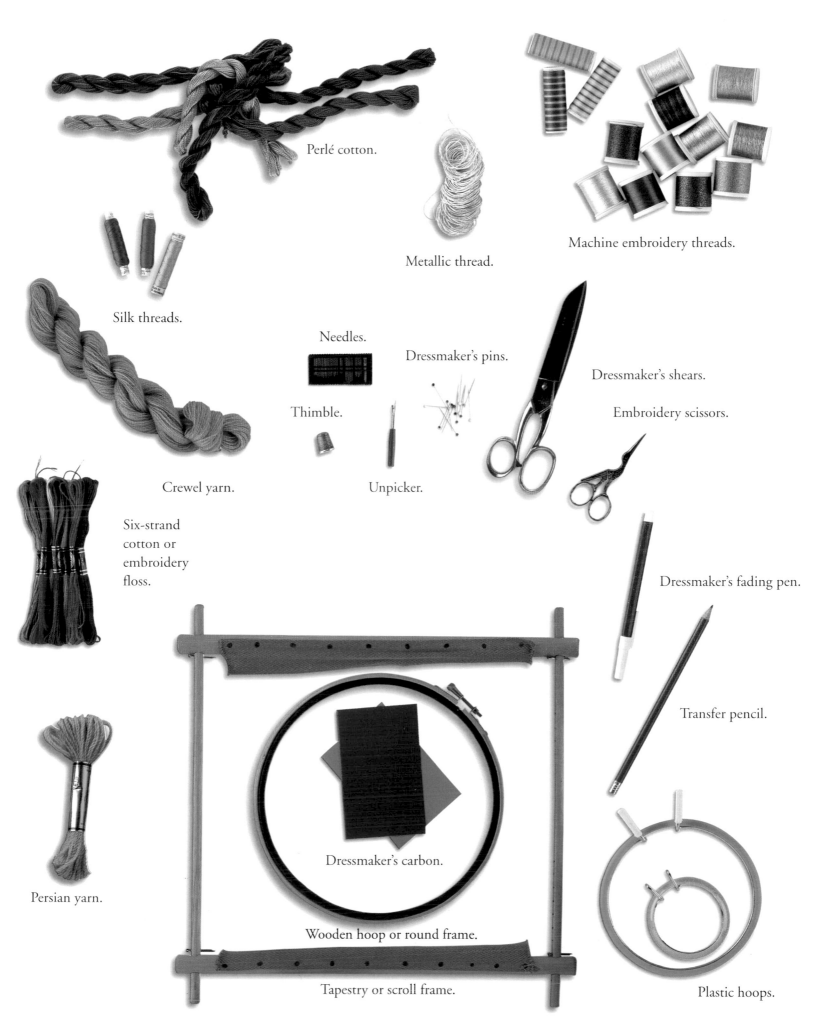

Perlé cotton.

Metallic thread.

Machine embroidery threads.

Silk threads.

Needles.

Dressmaker's pins.

Dressmaker's shears.

Thimble.

Embroidery scissors.

Crewel yarn.

Unpicker.

Six-strand cotton or embroidery floss.

Dressmaker's fading pen.

Transfer pencil.

Dressmaker's carbon.

Persian yarn.

Wooden hoop or round frame.

Tapestry or scroll frame.

Plastic hoops.

Starting Off

Most embroidery should be worked in a frame to allow an even stitch tension and to prevent the fabric becoming distorted. A tapestry frame is suitable for larger pieces of work but for small hand-stitched projects and all machine embroidery, a two-part hoop frame is used. To keep delicate fabrics taut, the inner ring can be bound with bias binding.

Right: Hoop frames are easy to manage and portable, and can be used for working larger pieces by changing the position when each area is completed, although this may cause distortion to finer embroidery.

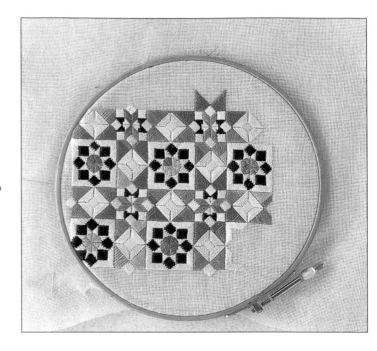

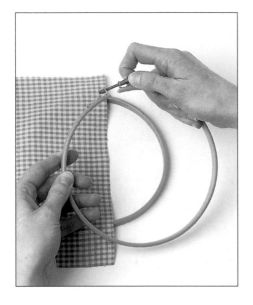

1 USING A FRAME To mount the cloth in the hoop, loosen the screw on the outer ring and separate the two parts. Place the fabric over the inner ring and press the outer ring down in place.

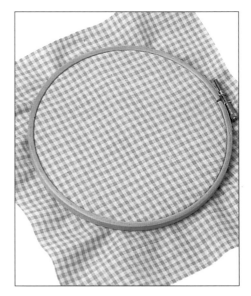

2 Stretch the fabric so that it is taut. Be sure that the weave lies squarely as shown. Tighten the screw. For machine embroidery the fabric should be right side up with the stitching area at the bottom of the hoop.

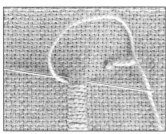

1 BEGINNING TO STITCH Working threads should not be longer than 45cm (18in) or they will fray and become tangled. The needle selected should always be the right size for the thread and fabric; a small eye can harm the thread, while a thick needle will leave large holes. Threads have a natural tendency to twist back on themselves; if this happens, let the needle and thread hang down and untwist. It is not advisable to anchor the thread with a knot at the back as it may distort the surface. Instead, when starting the first stitches of a piece, make a knot and insert the needle from the front, a short distance away from the area to be worked, so that the thread will be held fast at the back by the stitching. The knot can then be snipped off.

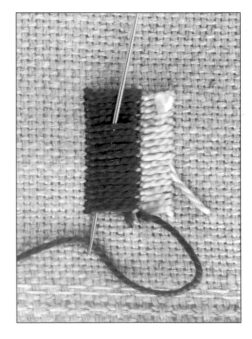

2 Subsequent threads can be started off by slipping the needle under the back of the existing stitches and working a back stitch. Finish off in the same way, and trim the loose ends.

Transferring and Charting

Patterns can be transferred on to a background in several ways; the choice depends on the nature of the design itself as well as the fabric and thread to be used. It is important that any lines marked should not show through the stitches; dressmaker's pens are now available which are either water-soluble or which fade completely over time. These are particularly suitable for fine freehand drawing or tracing directly on to the fabric via a light box. A chalk pencil can be used for bolder designs. Dressmaker's carbon paper is also used for indirect tracing and is best for smooth fabrics.

Right: The strawberry motif makes a perfect decoration for this ready-made lacy jam-pot cover.

1 TISSUE TACKING (BASTING) This is used for textured materials such as velvet, where a drawn line would not show. Trace the design on to tissue paper then pin to the right side of the fabric. With a contrasting thread, work over the design using a small running stitch.

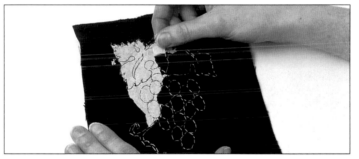

2 When complete, carefully tear away the tissue paper without pulling the thread. The embroidery is then worked over this guideline and any tacking (basting) which remains can be cut away.

TRANSFER PENCIL Using an embroidery transfer pencil and thin paper, trace the design. If the pattern is symmetrical or needs to be reversed, place the paper, with the pencil side down, on to the fabric, pin in place and press with a cool iron. For an outline which is the same as the original, trace it with a pencil, turn the paper and draw over the lines with the transfer pencil.

CROSS STITCH CHARTS The regular format of cross stitch makes it ideal for charting designs on to graph paper, where one square represents one stitch. Trace the design on to special tracing paper printed with a grid, as shown, or transfer it on to squared paper. Fill in the outline with coloured pens or pencils, to match the colours to be used.

Straight Stitches

There is an enormous variety of traditional stitches which provide the foundation for hand embroidery and sewing throughout the world. Some may be intricately textured or interwoven with precious gold thread; others use a simple row of stranded cotton to outline a design, or form twisted knots to make a single point of colour. All of them, however, are derived from three basic ways of working: straight, looped or knotted stitches. A wide range of textures and effects can be achieved just by using simple variations of flat, straight stitches. They can be worked in rows, at different angles and in varying sizes or combined to produce geometric shapes.

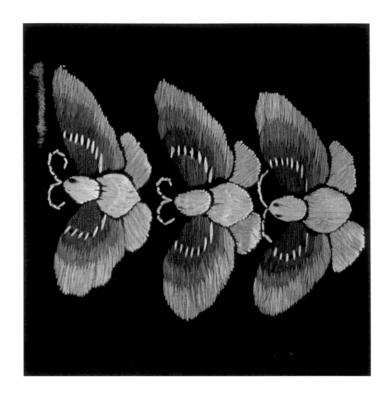

Right: These satin stitch butterflies were stitched with shiny silk thread on this piece of antique Chinese embroidery.

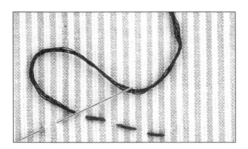

RUNNING STITCH This is the most basic of stitches, and is used to join pieces of fabric, outline motifs and for quilting. The stitches should all be equal in length and evenly spaced. A long running stitch is used for tacking (basting).

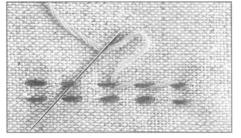

WHIP STITCH   A contrasting thread is woven through a basic line of running stitch to give a twisted effect to this stitch. Be careful not to pick up any of the background fabric.

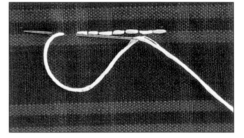

BACK STITCH This consists of a continuous line of even stitches. The needle is carried behind the work for twice the length of the finished stitch. It is used for outlines, especially in Assisi or blackwork.

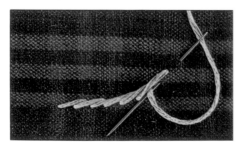

STEM STITCH Also known as crewel stitch, this is similar to back stitch. The thread should always lie to one side of the needle. The width can be altered by varying the stitch angle.

SEED STITCH Short detached stitches, all measuring the same length, are worked at random to produce a powdered filling, or to add pattern to a plain area. As a variation, two parallel stitches can be worked to give a more raised surface.

SATIN STITCH It may take some practice to achieve the distinctive smooth finish and tidy edge of this versatile stitch. The individual stitches, which should not be too long, are all worked in the same direction.

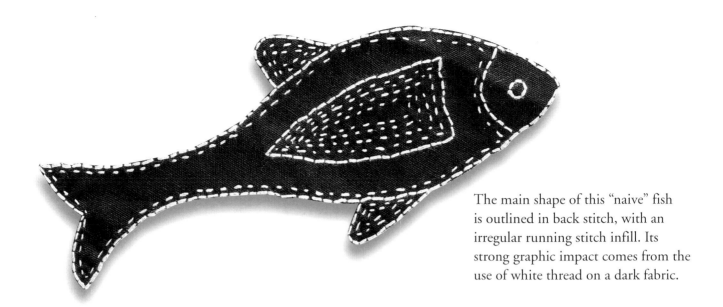

The main shape of this "naive" fish is outlined in back stitch, with an irregular running stitch infill. Its strong graphic impact comes from the use of white thread on a dark fabric.

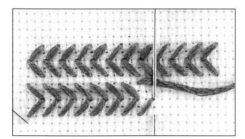

ARROWHEAD STITCH Two equal straight stitches at right angles form the arrow points, which can be evenly spaced in regular rows or worked as random individual stitches to give a scattered filling over a larger area.

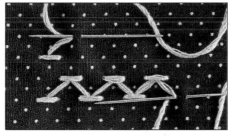

CHEVRON STITCH This looks particularly effective when worked on striped or spotted fabric. It is made up of a line of straight stitches worked at right angles to each other with a short back stitch at the intersection point.

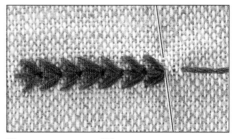

FERN STITCH This gives a leafy effect, which is ideal for plant designs. It is made up of three small stitches radiating from a point, and can be worked in straight or curved lines, or detached as a filling stitch.

This Indian bird is worked entirely in straight stitches and uses coloured cottons on a natural linen background. It is framed by a triple row of interlaced running stitch.

Cross Stitches

A basic cross stitch is formed by working one straight stitch across another. There are several variations where the angle of the cross is altered or the stitches overlap, and all can be worked in rows or singly. The regular pattern produced by all these stitches is ideally suited for embroidering on ginghams, striped fabrics or even-weave linen. Cross stitch is the foundation for the traditional embroidery of many cultures, from ancient Egyptian textiles to the geometric designs of modern Scandinavian work.

In the past, children learnt to sew by practising cross stitch samplers, and today a wide range of charted designs is available.

Narrow strips of even-weave fabric with decorative borders can be bought by length and are ideal for making small gift items such as bookmarks, decorative cake-ribbons or these monogrammed napkin rings.

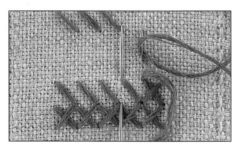

CROSS STITCH This stitch can be worked individually for outlines and letters, but is usually made in two separate rows, as shown, when a larger area has to be covered. The second line of stitches should always lie in the same direction for an even appearance.

HERRINGBONE STITCH This is often used to form a border around work and is particularly effective when stitched between two lines on a striped fabric. It is worked from left to right with an even space between the overlapping arms.

LACED HERRINGBONE STITCH Extra interest can be added to plain herringbone stitch by interlacing it with a contrasting colour. A blunt needle is used to prevent any of the foundation fabric getting caught up and the thread should not be pulled too tightly.

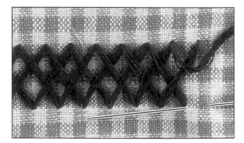

CLOSED HERRINGBONE STITCH This is worked as for herringbone but the space between the stitches is closed up. It is sometimes sewn on the reverse of a fine fabric so that the front gives the appearance of two lines of back stitch and the diagonal stitches are visible through the cloth. This technique is known as "shadow work".

DOUBLE HERRINGBONE STITCH To produce an interlaced effect, the needle is passed down and below the upward stitches on the first row, so that they all lie above the downward stitches. The second row uses a contrasting colour, and is worked in the same way, with the upward stitches threaded under the downward stitches of the first row.

LONGARM CROSS STITCH This overlapping stitch produces a dense, braided finish and is useful for heavy outlines. It is worked from left to right, with a longer and more slanted second arm and the diagonals meet at the top and bottom.

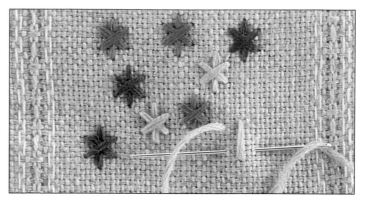

DOUBLE CROSS STITCH This star-shaped stitch can be worked individually or in lines. It is made up of two simple cross stitches worked one over the other.

ERMINE FILLING An upright straight stitch is overlapped with a single cross stitch to produce a six-pointed star, which can be repeated at random or in regular rows for a more formal effect.

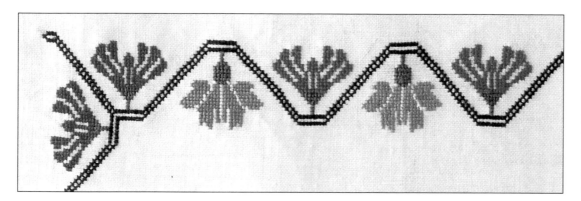

Left: The cross stitch samplers of the nineteenth century were embroidered with alphabets, mottoes and pictorial motifs. This typical carnation border is a combination of both geometric and floral elements.

Right: This lavender sachet is made from Aida cloth, a woven fabric which is produced especially for cross stitch work. It is easy to use, as there is no need for complicated thread counting, and is available in a range of sizes and colours.

Assisi Work

This historic variation originated in the Italian town of Assisi. It reverses the usual method of working cross stitch patterns – with striking results. The main motifs are first outlined with a single line and the background filled in with solid rows of cross stitch. The stylized imagery is based on birds, fish and animals – both real and mythical – along with geometric and floral motifs. It underwent a revival in the early 1900s, when the old patterns were redrawn. It is traditionally worked on cream or white even-weave linen, using a combination of red, blue and black embroidery threads.

Right: This heraldic dragon is worked in black against red and edged with a Greek key pattern. Single stitches emphasize the claws and the eye is marked with a detached cross stitch.

On a much smaller scale, these two ducks (above) were adapted from a pattern card, published in the early twentieth century when there was a great renewal of interest in Assisi work.

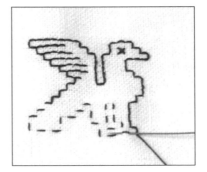

1 Work the motif and border with Holbein stitch, which resembles back stitch. This is sewn as two rounds of running stitch, the second row filling the spaces left between the first.

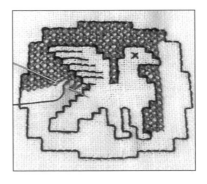

2 The background is completely filled with cross stitch, in a bright primary colour. The stitches can be worked singly, or, as is usual with this technique, back and forth in rows.

3 The elaborate linear border is worked in Holbein stitch, using the main colour again.

Blackwork

Blackwork uses straight and back stitches to create small-scale all-over patterns. This distinctive embroidery became popular in sixteenth-century England, when it was used to decorate caps, gloves, sleeves and bodices. Design at that time was naturalistic; the geometric repeats of blackwork were worked to fill in the flowing outlines of flower petals, leaves and fruit. It is traditionally done using stranded cotton on even-weave linen, but Aida cloth provides a quicker alternative.

Right: Different patterns all have their own tonal value, ranging from dark to light, depending on how the stitches are arranged. This sampler features some old and new variations (clockwise from top right): *Algerian eye stitch* consists of eight straight stitches radiating from a central point; *Zigzag stitch* is worked in diagonal rows of stepped back stitch; *Fishscale stitch* is built up in rows of short straight stitches, linked with a zigzag; *Shoofly stitch* consists of four triangles arranged at the points of a cross stitch; *Grid stitch* consists of separate motifs, which may be joined with diagonal back stitches; *Pinwheel stitch* is worked in back stitch as a series of individual shapes*; Square stitch*, a half-drop repeat, can be made singly or by working rows of running stitch; and *Lattice stitch* is a deceptively simple pattern of interlocking diamonds and squares.

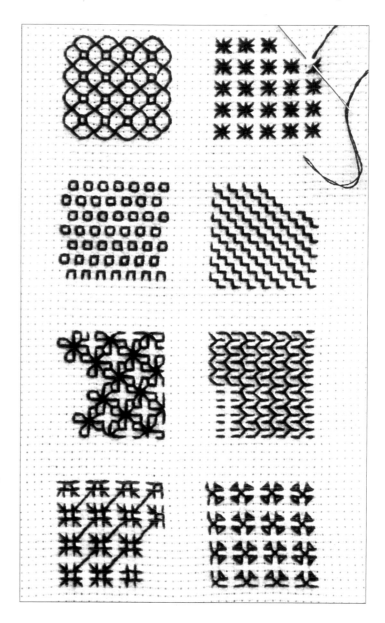

There is an infinite array of geometric patterns that can be used for blackwork (above). Any tiny shape can be adapted by charting it on to graph paper and working out a repeat. The border of a fragment of broken pottery was the inspiration for this series of single motifs and all-over fillings.

The symmetry of blackwork means that the most basic computer graphics package can be used to produce suitable patterns. This computer-designed example (left) has the appearance of a piece of very traditional work, but is, in fact, a marriage of old and new.

17

Looped and Knotted Stitches

Instead of simply sewing in and out of the background as for the previous stitches, the stitches in this group are all formed by looping the thread and holding it down on the surface, either with further stitches, or by passing the needle through the thread to form a knot. Variations range from functional blanket stitch to the raised textures of bullion and French knots. Chain and feather stitches can be worked quickly and produce a decorative effect, which is popular for "crazy" patchwork. It is important that all of these stitches are worked with an even tension and that the loops are not pulled tightly.

Above: This Indian marriage cloth is embroidered with a variety of stitches, which includes rows of closely worked chain stitch to define squares and chevrons.

CHAIN STITCHES

Chain stitch
Pass the needle down and under the fabric for the correct length and pull through, keeping the thread tucked below the point. Work the next stitch through the loop, into the hole where the thread emerged.

Threaded chain stitch A row of evenly spaced detached chain stitches forms the foundation for this double link chain. Each one is secured below the loop with a small stitch. A contrasting thread is threaded under the loops in each direction.

Lazy daisy stitch Single chain stitches are sewn in the round to form this popular flower shape. Each flower should be arranged evenly in a circle and worked from the centre out. Further single stitches can be used to make leaves.

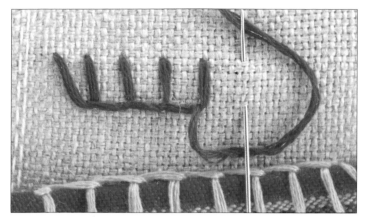

Blanket stitch This can be worked as an edging or surface stitch, or closely together for buttonholes. It is worked from left to right, in a row of regular upright stitches, with the thread always passing under the needle.

Feather stitch This is worked from top to bottom as a series of alternate slanting stitches. Again, the thread always lies under the needle to form the characteristic loops. It is often used in conjunction with smocking.

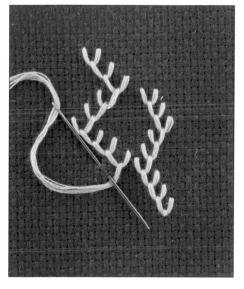

Double feather stitch This border stitch is an elaboration of the basic feather stitch. Two stitches, instead of one, are made to one side and then to the other. It can be varied by changing the angle.

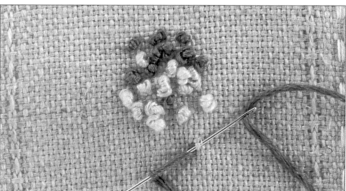

KNOTTED STITCHES *French knot* Bring the needle out and hold the thread taut. Wrap it twice round the needle and tighten the thread. Push the needle back through the fabric, close to the point from which it emerged.

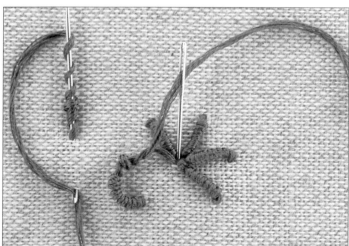

Bullion knot The method is similar to the French knot. Start off with a back stitch of the required length. Wrap the thread round several times and hold it down as the needle is pulled carefully through the loops and inserted back at the start.

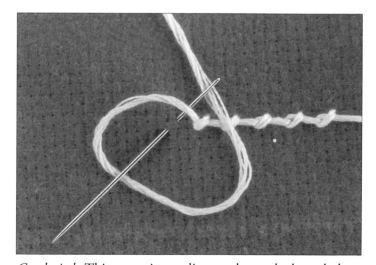

Coral stitch This attractive outline can be worked regularly or so that the knots are spaced at random. Pass the needle through a small amount of fabric at an angle, looping the thread over the needle and pulling through to form a knot.

19

Whitework

1 With a dressmaker's pen or soft pencil, draw round the leaf on to the background fabric.

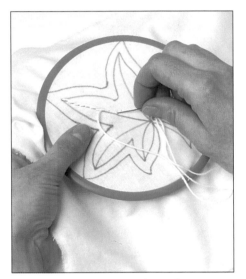

2 Thread a large-eyed needle with crochet cotton and work the veins in stem or back stitch.

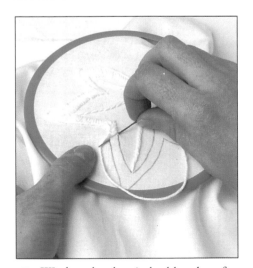

3 Work a closely stitched border of satin or blanket stitch around the outline, and pick out the stalk in stem stitch.

Whitework is a generic term for the many types of white-on-white embroidery, unlike blackwork which describes a single, specialized technique. It is most often used on household linens: tray or tablecloths, pillow covers, nightdress cases, lingerie and handkerchiefs. Variations include the delicate floral Scottish Ayrshire Work, the traditional decoration for christening gowns, Norwegian Hardanger stitchery and the open lace work of *broderie anglaise* (eyelet lace). Mountmellick work is the Irish version of whitework, named after the town in which it was first developed. It is worked in a variety of raised and textured stitches, using a matt (non-shiny) crochet-type thread on a cotton drill (twill) background. Like much other whitework, it draws on the natural imagery of plants, fruit and flowers, but interprets it in a bold, graphic style. It was used to make articles that varied in scale from babies' bibs and collars to bedspreads. Special pattern books and transfers were also produced. A contemporary and personal interpretation is to collect interestingly shaped leaves – from the garden or from a country walk – to use as templates.

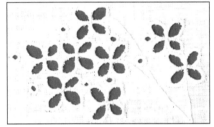

This *broderie anglaise* (eyelet lace) sprig was worked by outlining the petals with a narrow satin stitch, then cutting away the surplus fabric to form the distinctive eyelets.

Right: A delicate handkerchief was once an essential accessory; this lace-edged antique example is densely embroidered with the owner's initials and a deep border. It is stitched in cotton on a fine lawn ground.

Pulled and Drawn Thread Work

These two techniques are used to create delicate lace-like effects on fine, even-weave fabrics. They have long been classified as whitework, but they can look very dramatic if done in coloured threads or on a patterned fabric. In pulled work the stitches are worked tightly so that the threads of the fabric are forced apart to create a pattern, whereas in drawn thread work threads are removed from the foundation fabric for a more open look.

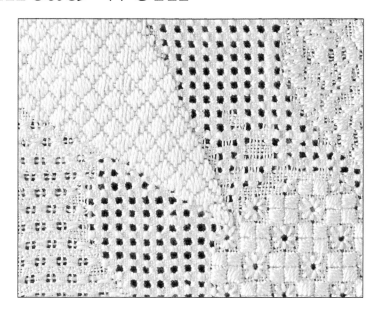

Right: Interesting areas of texture can be produced by experimenting with the many pulled thread stitches, as in this abstract sampler.

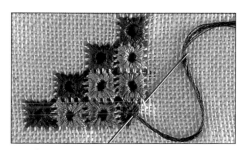

1 PULLED THREAD STITCHES
Algerian eye stitch This open eyelet is formed by working 16 straight stitches, radiating from a central point. It can be worked singly or in rows.

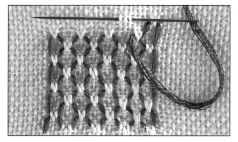

2 *Honeycomb darning* This regular open background stitch is worked over three threads, in rows from right to left, then left to right.

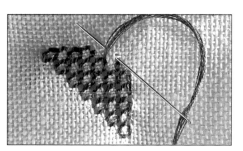

3 *Single faggot stitch* This filling stitch is worked in stepped diagonal rows, which build up to form a grid.

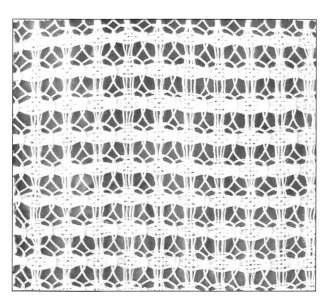

Above: Beautiful all-over patterns can be produced by working in white thread on white linen. The intricacy of this design is emphasized by a backing of hand-dyed silk.

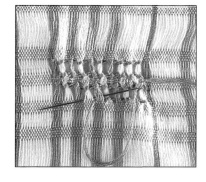

1 DRAWN THREAD STITCHES
Ladder stitch These simple examples are worked on loosely woven checked linen, from which bands of thread were removed. Back stitch is used to pull the remaining threads into clusters.

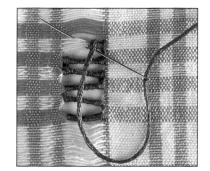

2 *Corded clusters* Solid clusters are made by binding the embroidery thread tightly around groups of foundation threads.

Couching and Laid Thread Work

Couching and laid thread work are two closely related techniques which have been used for centuries when embroidering with textured, silk floss and metallic threads, or narrow cords and ribbons that cannot be drawn through the background fabric. Instead, these threads are attached to the surface with tiny straight or ornamental stitches worked in a finer thread. Couching is a fast and effective way to define curves, outlines and decorative spirals, while laid thread work is generally used to fill motifs and to cover backgrounds. An embroidery frame should always be used for these techniques, to prevent the stitches from puckering. Neither thread should be pulled too tightly or the shapes will distort.

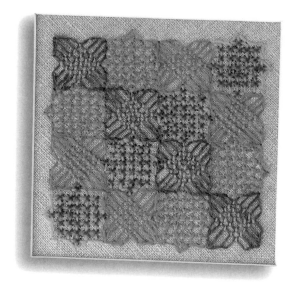

Above: The motifs of this panel are worked in several filling stitches, and show the depth and texture that can be created.

COUCHING *Plain couching* Place the thread to be couched in the position required on the fabric. Make small detached stitches at regular intervals to anchor it down, in a contrasting thread. Tidy the piece by drawing the loose ends to the back of the fabric.

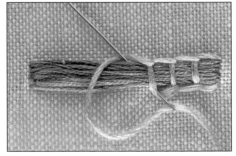

Decorative couching Embroidery stitches such as cross stitch or blanket stitch can be used to secure the laid thread for a more decorative effect. Here square chain stitch is worked through the fabric, across several strands of cotton.

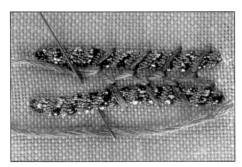

Double couching Two parallel lines of broad metallic thread are held down by a row of feather stitch, with half of the feather stitch being worked over each line of metallic thread.

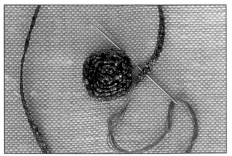

Spiral couching To fill a circle, bring both threads up in the centre of the circle. Coil the thread to be couched in a spiral, and couch down with the other thread at regular intervals to form a spoked pattern.

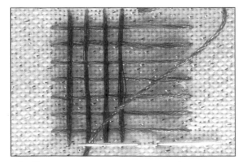

1 LAID WORK *Lattice work* Large areas or individual shapes can be covered with this filling stitch. The basic lattice is made by working rows of long parallel stitches, both horizontally and vertically, to form a regular grid.

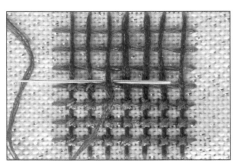

2 Small contrasting stitches are worked over each thread intersection to secure the long threads to the background and to decorate the grid. Further patterning can be added by working extra stitches within the squares.

Left: This jewel-like patchwork has been assembled from fragments of antique gold and mirror work from northern India. A variety of couching techniques has been used to create the geometric patterns.

Right: Contrasting couched threads have been used to emphasize the outline of these simple animal figures, and to disguise the edges of the appliquéd shapes.

Above: These luxurious and innovative samples use a range of couched techniques, including a spiral of silver wire which is held in place with almost invisible stitches.

Machine Embroidery

Machine embroidery is innovative, quick to work and growing in popularity. Sewing machines have always been used to produce decorative effects, as well as for plain stitching, but the swing-needle machine has great potential as a creative tool. The latest generation of electronic machines is increasingly sophisticated and comes complete with pre-programmed patterns, alphabets and even the capability of scanning in designs. Despite this, exciting effects can still be achieved with the simple straight and zigzag stitches of the standard domestic machine. The instruction manual will have details of any special embroidery feet or attachments which have been supplied and it should be consulted for information about basic stitching methods. Starting to work in this unfamiliar way may seem a little daunting at first, so take time to become familiar with how the machine works and don't be afraid to experiment. Always stitch at the slowest speed and do not race the machine.

FREE STITCHING
For normal use the machine stitch is controlled by the "feed dog" which produces an even stitch by regulating the pace at which the fabric goes under the presser foot. If this is lowered or covered (depending on the machine model – check the manual for details of how to do this) the stitch can be controlled by moving the fabric in the desired direction.

The background and main blocks of plain colour in these amusing illustrations have been filled in with multi-directional satin stitch in varying widths, with the fine details worked in straight stitch.

SATIN STITCH The fabric should be kept taut in a frame, and held lightly with both hands. Thread the machine as normal and set the controls to zigzag. Apply gentle pressure to the pedal and move the frame slowly forwards so that a close satin stitch is built up. The width can be varied by adjusting the controls.

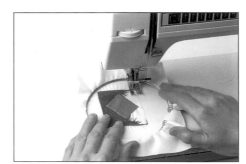

1 STRAIGHT STITCH Lines of straight stitch can be worked in exactly the same way as satin stitch, and if they are made in different directions, interesting textures can be created. The frame can be moved from side to side or back and forth.

2 With practice and experiment, curved and wavy lines can be easily achieved. These are best sewn at a gentle speed so that the background can be manipulated below the presser foot.

Machine embroidery need not be limited to the usual fabrics; the baroque picture frames which surround these batik figures are made from dyed heavyweight interfacing.

Layers of straight stitch can be built up to create a great depth of colour and interest within a piece of work, as in these dynamic portraits of African women.

Once the basic methods have been mastered, machine embroidery can become a very flexible way of "drawing"; this notebook contains a series of experimental images which include more advanced techniques such as changing the tension of either the top or bobbin threads to produce irregular, looped stitches.

25

Working on a Painted Background

Machine embroidery can be used to produce a free outline, which is as flexible as a hand-drawn line. Straight stitch is particularly useful for adding detail to and defining a design, which may be painted on material with fabric paints or with watercolours, gouache or acrylics on to paper.

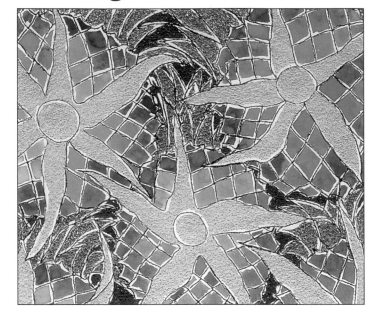

Right: The colours and shapes of a pineapple inspired this lively tropical design. The yellow stars are given an added dynamism by the diamond shapes that surround them.

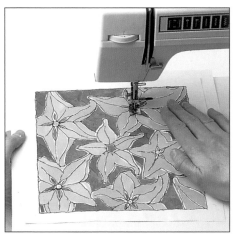

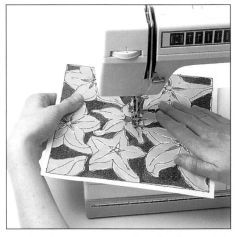

1 Choose a design which has clear areas of colour and a strong outline and paint it on to heavy paper; watercolour paper is ideal. Mount the design onto a second, slightly larger, piece of paper for extra support.

2 Thread the machine with black cotton and stitch slowly around the outlines. These can be emphasized by working twice over some areas.

3 Fill in various blocks of colour with a free zigzag stitch, using a thread that is a shade darker than the painted background to give a feeling of depth.

Left: This linen placemat was made in the 1950s, at the time when machine embroidery was first being explored as an art form. It is worked in straight stitch on a screen-printed background.

Working with Paper

Paper can be used like fabric as a background for machine embroidery, but it can also be put to many other uses. It can be painted, torn or cut into shapes and interwoven with ribbons to create interesting multi-layered and collage effects. Be sure that the stitch tension is not too tight when working on paper as it can easily tear.

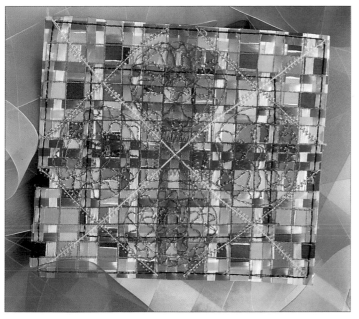

Above: For this colourful example, bright lines of straight stitch have been sewn to run parallel with the weave. These contrast with the floral motifs sewn on to the surface.

Above: This illustration was made by gluing torn paper shapes on to a plain background, then "drawing" on the black lines in free straight stitch.

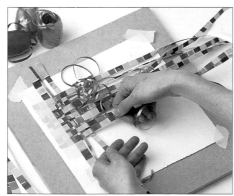

1 WOVEN PAPER WITH RIBBONS
Find some gift ribbons and paint cartridge paper with bands of colour to match. Cut into narrow strips and arrange horizontally with the ribbons on the backing paper. Fix with masking tape along one side and interweave the vertical pieces.

2 When the work is the desired size, tape the edges to hold the paper and ribbons in place for stitching.

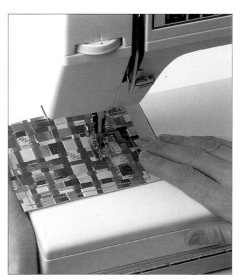

3 Stitch through the backing, the woven strips and ribbon around the outer edge, then free stitch over the surface in a variety of colours.

Machine Lace

Machine lace fabrics are constructed by building up a network of interlocking stitches on a specially produced background material, which is then removed to leave an open web of thread. This is done by applying heat or by dissolving it in water. There are three different fabrics available, each with special qualities. The working method is the same for all three, however: the rows of stitching must always intersect and cross each other so that the finished piece retains its shape. For extra flexibility in stitching, the presser foot can be taken off. This means that the fabric can be moved in a freer way. It is worth taking time to become familiar with this way of working, by practising on a frame stretched with fine cotton. The hoop must always be held at the outer rim to avoid accidents.

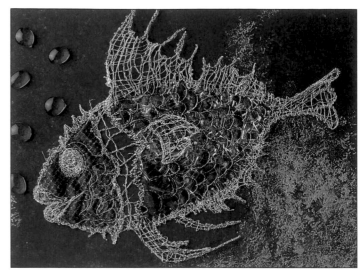

Above: The fins and tail of this exotic fish are worked in a mesh of metallic threads and the glittering body is formed from tiny scraps of shiny fabric and glitter which have been trapped between two layers of bronze organza (organdy).

1 MULTILAYERED WATER-SOLUBLE METHOD Stretch the fabric tautly in a hoop and trace the outline with a felt-tip pen. Use a size 9 needle and thread the machine with metallic machine embroidery thread. Drop or cover the feed dog, set the stitch length to zero, then sew over and within the shape to form a tracery of thread. To create extra colour, add small cuttings of thread and net between two pieces of organza (organdy) and stitch over.

2 Rinse the finished piece in a bowl of water or directly under the cold tap. The backing fabric will simply disappear and all traces can be washed away.

3 Blot the work between layers of paper towel and ease into shape. Leave to dry away from any direct heat.

4 An extra dimension can be added by stiffening the piece with spray varnish. It can then be moulded or shaped and left to dry.

VANISHING MUSLIN is a stiffened loose-weave material which is worked in a frame then pressed under a cloth with a hot iron or put in a pre-warmed oven at 300°F/150°C for five minutes. The heat causes the fibres to discolour and disintegrate.

COLD-WATER-SOLUBLE FABRIC is made from a natural fibre which is a derivative of seaweed. It is delicate and must be worked in a hoop. It is not suitable for very dense sewing – although a double layer can be used if stitching closely – but it is ideal for creating fine multilayered textures, incorporating fragments of decorative cloth and fibre.

HOT-WATER-SOLUBLE FABRIC is stronger and stiffer than the cold-water version. It is used for heavier stitching and can be worked without a frame. The finished piece is then boiled for five minutes in a saucepan of water to dissolve the backing, and then stretched back into shape as it dries.

Above: Tiny pearls and fine lace have been used to decorate the golden machine lace garments worn by this ethereal fairy.

Below: These dramatic large-scale figures each measure 45cm (18in) high. The embroidery has been worked directly over the wire frames which support them, on a backing of water-soluble fabric, to create a wide range of intricate patterns and textures.

Right: The jewel-like effect of metallic machine lace makes it particularly suitable for use in small projects such as earrings. Special jewellery findings are available from most craft stores.

Needlepoint

The popular craft of needlepoint is also known as tapestry, canvas work and canvas embroidery. The formal stitches are worked on to a geometric canvas grid, using various scales; stranded embroidery silks on fine canvas give a lustrous, detailed result, while several strands of woollen yarn can be worked together on a thick rug canvas.

The first large pieces of needlepoint were made in imitation of the expensive and sought-after tapestries that were hand-woven in specialist workshops in Britain and Europe. They were worked in a single stitch on fine canvas to give the appearance of the densely woven texture of true tapestry, and some of the stitch names, such as "Gobelin filling", after the French tapestry studio, reflect this. The most popular stitch was tent stitch, and this is still most commonly used for pictorial work, particularly ready-to-work kits. It produces a durable surface, which can last for many years.

Needlepoint has always been the most practical form of embroidery and the most hard-wearing, which means that much of it has survived the centuries. The ornamental court dress and other embroidered clothing of the

A carefully thought-out selection of needlepoint stitches has been used to embroider this classically proportioned house, its garden and its background.

Elizabethan era was recycled when it became unfashionable. Pearls, beads and jewels were reused, gold thread was taken out and tassels unravelled. Many needlepoint items from that time, however, were preserved, including panels believed to have been worked by the Queen herself. Bible covers, often featuring scenes from the Old and New Testaments, were made to protect precious printed books from wear, and purses or bags were made as gifts. These often featured mottoes, along with the emblematic and symbolic devices that fascinated the Elizabethans.

Illustrated pattern books first appeared on the market in sixteenth century Europe, and these provided a vast resource for professional and amateur designers. One of the earliest has the engaging title: *A Book of Beasts, Birds, Flowers, Fruits, Flies and Wormes, exactly drawne with their Lively Colours truly Described,* which gives a graphic impression of the outline designs contained in it. Samplers were often made to try out some of these patterns, but the early versions were purely practice pieces worked on long strips of fabric, not framed for display, like later work.

In addition to small items,

Ready-made kits, such as this duck cushion (pillow), are screen printed on to canvas. A separate screen is made for each of the colours in the design and the inks carefully matched to the yarns.

that could not have been achieved with natural dyes. Many of the old charts have survived and give some idea of just how bright Victorian needlework really was. The colours have faded over the years, and many antique pieces have a worn and nostalgic look that belies their original appearance.

Ladies of leisure set about adorning their homes with bell-pulls, footstools, firescreens and pictures and making smoking caps, braces (suspenders) and slippers for their menfolk. Patterns ranged from representational romantic landscapes, through realistic bowls of flowers to outrightly sentimental portraits of the royal princes and princesses and even the Queen's pets. Some of the designs were very complicated and intricate and the Countess of Wilton, writing in 1840, bemoaned the fact that many women optimistically bought charts and yarns, then found that they could not easily work them – a not uncommon complaint today.

Tent stitch pictures will always be popular, but needlepoint has now evolved into an independent branch of embroidery, with many stitches – both traditional and modern variations – which can be combined to give an enormous range of effects, patterns, styles and textures.

This modern reworking of an antique charted pattern gives some impression of just how bright Victorian needlework was originally meant to be.

needlepoint was widely used for furnishings, from wall hangings and bed draperies to cushion (pillow) covers and footstools. In the days before padded upholstery, when all furniture was made from wood, soft cushions (pillows) were a necessary comfort. Floor coverings and rugs were also made, although these were not intended for everyday use, and special table carpets were made to drape over dining tables when not in use. These furnishings, usually worked in tent stitch, were decorated with biblical or mythical scenes and drew heavily on heraldic imagery. Trade links between the East and Europe were growing throughout the seventeenth century and as new and exotic textiles were imported, their designs were adapted for needlepoint.

For many years, needlepoint was used simply to copy paintings and engravings. It was not until the nineteenth century that it came into its own with the spread of Berlin woolwork. This was worked in cross or tent stitch from printed charts, which first appeared in Germany in 1805. Black and white engravings, which used

tiny symbols to represent different yarns, were hand-painted to give a full range of colour. Small numbers of designs were imported during the early years of the nineteenth century but it was with the invention of the first chemical or aniline dyes in the mid-nineteenth century that Berlin woolwork became widely popular. New textile technology meant that, for the first time, yarns could be manufactured in vivid hues – purple, emerald, crimson, lime greens and acid yellows –

Fruit, acorn, butterfly and flower motifs from an Elizabethan pattern book were the inspiration for this enchanting tent stitch design.

Needlepoint
Tools and Materials

Needlepoint, or canvas work, is the craft of stitching on to a firm open-weave square mesh or canvas, as opposed to the softer background fabrics used for embroidery. It is traditionally worked with wool, although many different yarns can be used to produce interesting effects.

THREADS
4-ply tapestry and 2-ply crewel yarns are both available in skeins or hanks, in a full range of colours. Vivid Persian yarn comes in three separate strands which can be divided.

CANVAS
Like embroidery linen, canvas is gauged by the number of threads that make up 2.5cm (1in): 10-count canvas is used for most tent stitch, rug canvas has just three squares to 2.5cm (1in) and fine 22-count fabric is used with single crewel yarns. Light-coloured canvas is suitable for working with pale colours, but antique or undyed canvas should be chosen for darker yarns so that it does not show through.

Mono, or single-thread canvas is available in a wide range of gauges for traditional needlepoint: for best results use interlock canvas which has a twisted warp and therefore does not pull out of shape easily. Double, or Penelope canvas is woven with pairs of thread, for tramming, which can also be sub-divided for areas of smaller stitching. Plastic canvas is sold by the sheet and can be cut to shape with scissors. It does not distort and is ideal for making three-dimensional shapes.

TOOLS AND ACCESSORIES
To avoid large pieces of work becoming distorted, a rectangular stretcher frame or an adjustable scroll frame must be used to mount the canvas. For smaller projects, the canvas can be simply bound with masking tape to prevent it unravelling and, if necessary, blocked into shape when complete.

A tapestry needle has a large eye for easy threading and a blunt point to pass between the canvas threads. Tapestry needles come in different sizes ranging from number 13 for coarse work, to the most common, number 20, down to the finest, number 25.

Both large and small scissors will be needed to cut canvas and yarns and a marker pen or acrylic paints are used to transfer designs directly on to the working canvas.

Persian yarns.

Crewel and tapestry yarns.

Embroidery scissors.   Acrylic paints with paint mixer.

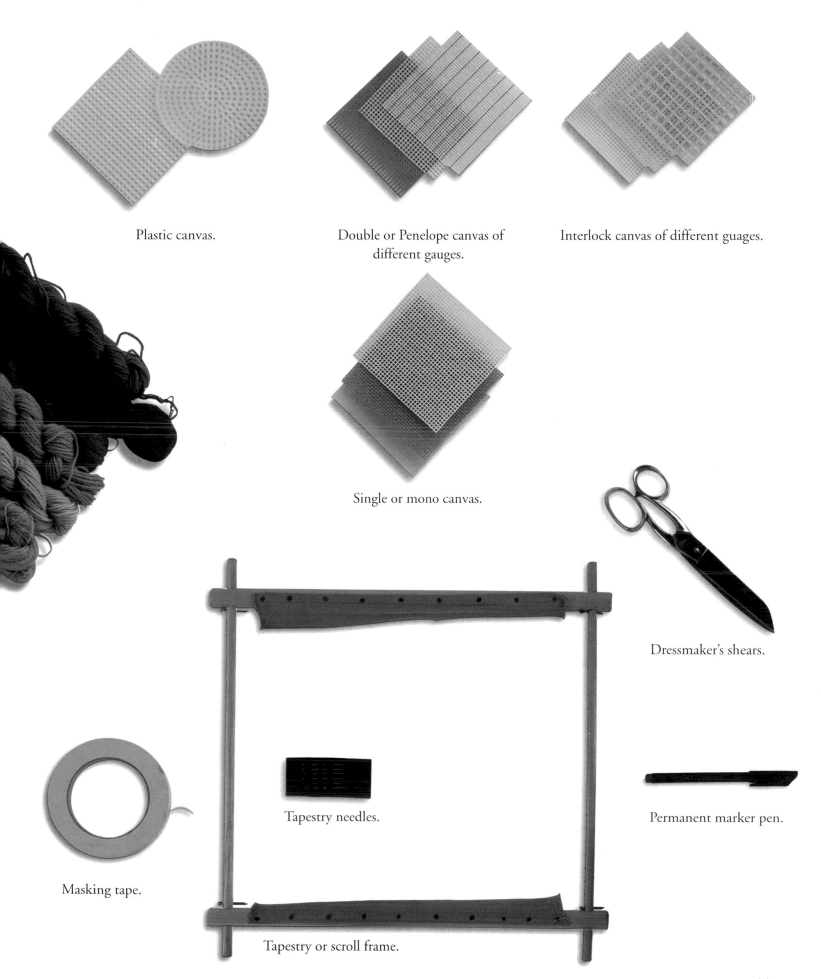

Plastic canvas.

Double or Penelope canvas of different gauges.

Interlock canvas of different guages.

Single or mono canvas.

Dressmaker's shears.

Tapestry needles.

Permanent marker pen.

Masking tape.

Tapestry or scroll frame.

Creating the Design

The scope for creating new designs is unlimited. Visual inspiration is all around: a single motif from a furnishing fabric can be adapted to make a co-ordinating cushion (pillow), or used on a smaller scale as an all-over repeat; a photograph of an exotic flower may suggest a representational tent stitch picture or a more abstract colour pattern, worked in textured stitches. It is important to bear in mind the scale of the finished piece – for a fast result, bold shapes can be worked on 7-count canvas with three strands of Persian yarn, but for fine detail 12- or 14-count canvas should be used with crewel or tapestry wool. Try combining stitches: tent stitch is good for details and fine lines, while decorative stitches will cover background areas more quickly.

DRAWING ON TO CANVAS

This Gothic Revival pattern has been traced directly on to the canvas, using a waterproof felt-tip pen. The canvas should be placed directly over the drawing. Be sure that the design is squared up correctly. This can be done by ruling horizontal and vertical guides to indicate the centre of the canvas and matching them with similar lines marked on the design. Tape the canvas in place before starting to draw.

1 MAKING CHARTS
The regular grid of graph paper resembles the mesh of woven canvas, which makes charting an ideal way to produce accurate needlepoint designs. It is particularly good for tent stitch patterns, where one coloured square represents one stitch. Match the scale of the paper to the canvas for easier working, e.g., 12-count paper to 12-count canvas.

PAINTING ON TO CANVAS

Highly detailed designs can be painted directly on to canvas using textile paints, which are then ironed to fix the colour. This technique works best on "antique" canvas which is made of unbleached fibres.

2 Choose a design that has a strong shape and solid blocks of colour. Trace the outline with a soft pencil and transfer on to graph paper.

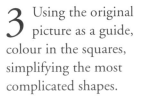

3 Using the original picture as a guide, colour in the squares, simplifying the most complicated shapes.

Working with Colour

Almost any type of thread can be used for needlepoint. Metallic yarns and silk floss provide highlights within a design; heavy-duty rug yarn is suitable for large-scale canvases, and perlé or stranded embroidery threads give a smooth lustrous texture. Woollen yarns are, however, the most popular choice, especially for items that will receive a lot of wear. A wide range of colours is available, from several specialist manufacturers. The yarn is spun from specially selected fibres, which make it more durable than knitting wool. Needlepoint wools come in three main types: tapestry yarn, crewel wool and Persian yarn. The first is a 4-ply single-strand yarn, supplied in skeins or larger hanks, which is used on medium canvases: Crewel wool is a 2-ply single strand yarn and can be worked singly on fine-mesh canvas for the most detailed work, or with several strands combined. Four strands are the equivalent of tapestry yarn. Persian yarn is also 2-ply and consists of three fine strands, which can easily be separated. The thread chosen for any work must cover the canvas threads completely without being so thick that it cannot be pulled through easily. Sew with a length of about 45cm (18in) to prevent the yarn becoming frayed or knotted.

1 By combining several separate strands of either crewel or Persian yarn, an infinite number of hues can be created. This can give depth to a representational image or, as here, be an excuse to work in bands of pure colour. The selection of yarns is based on the richly shaded landscape of the Channel Islands.

2 To blend the colours, cut equal lengths from the skeins and separate the strands.

3 Thread the needle with two contrasting or closely shaded yarns and work as usual. Up to four strands can be used on wider-mesh canvases; if all of these are different, some stunning results can be produced.

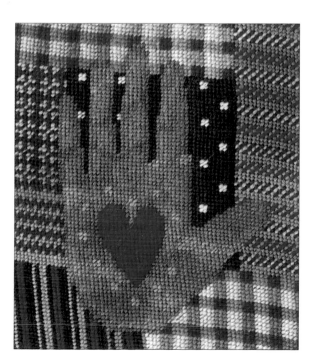

Left: The patterns on well-worn cotton print fabrics are the inspiration for this patchwork hand and heart. The subtle faded colours are reproduced by working with closely matched shades of Persian tapestry yarns.

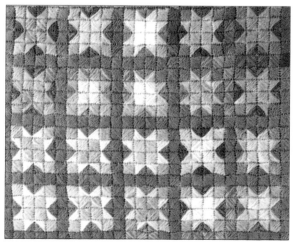

This simple geometric design is based on the Saw-tooth Star quilt motif and worked in two strands of crewel yarn on a fine canvas. The changes in colour give a lively appearance to the pattern surface.

Starting and Finishing

Needlepoint's popularity comes from the fact that only the most basic equipment is needed, there are no special techniques to be learned and it is quick to work. The yarn must be started and ended correctly, and an even tension maintained. This will come with experience, so it is worth practising a few stitches on spare canvas.

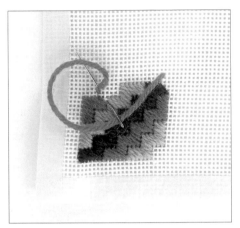

1 PREPARING THE CANVAS The canvas should be bound with masking tape to prevent the edges unravelling and to stop the yarn from catching. If a frame is not being used, the sides of a large piece of work can be rolled up, so that only the area being stitched shows.

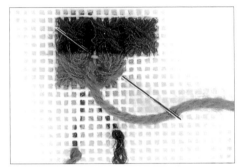

3 GETTING STARTED The end of the wool should not simply be knotted and pulled to the right side, as in embroidery, because it can easily become untied or work through the canvas. Instead the needle is passed through from the front, a short distance from the starting point, then brought up from the back. When the surplus yarn has been stitched over, the knot can be snipped off.

2 FINISHING OFF The yarn is finished on the wrong side. Bring the needle through and weave it under the back of the finished stitches for about 2.5cm (1in). Trim the end. Try not to start and end the threads in the same place: this can make the work uneven.

BLOCKING

Most needlepoint stitches are diagonal, so the square weave of the canvas is bound to get pulled out of line during sewing. This is less likely to happen if the work has been supported on a frame, but some distortion is inevitable. The finished piece should be very lightly pressed from the wrong side with a steam iron, but may need to be "blocked" to restore its intended shape.

1 Dampen the work thoroughly on both sides, using a water spray.

2 Place a protective piece of plastic under the canvas, then pin down the first corner. Stretch the canvas and secure the opposite corner. Pull the work into shape and pin down the other two corners.

3 Push more drawing pins (thumb tacks) into the unstitched canvas, and use a ruler or set square to check the right angles at each corner. Leave to dry away from any direct source of heat.

Tent Stitch

Tent stitch, sometimes known as petit point, is the most flexible of all needlepoint stitches. It produces an even texture, and can be worked in large blocks of solid colour or used for shading effects and fine detail. It is worked diagonally, with all the stitches lying in the same direction. There are three different ways of forming the stitch: half cross stitch, continental stitch and basketweave stitch.

HALF CROSS STITCH

This must be worked on double or interlocked canvas to prevent the stitches slipping. Although it resembles continental stitch from the front, half cross stitch is worked quite differently, and using both stitches in one piece gives an irregular surface.

1 Start at the top left and work each row from left to right. Bring the needle through and take it up to the right over one intersection, then back down under one horizontal thread and out to start the next stitch.

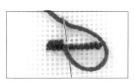

2 Turn the canvas upside down, and work the next row in the same way.

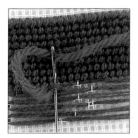

TRAMMED TENT STITCH
Worked on double thread canvas, over a long foundation stitch, this method gives a slightly ridged and very resilient surface, which is traditionally used for stools or chair seats.

Left: Cushion (pillow) covers, which need to be hard-wearing, are usually worked in tent stitch.

The reverse of these canvases shows the differences between the three methods of working tent stitch. Left to right: half cross stitch, continental stitch, basketweave stitch.

CONTINENTAL STITCH
This second horizontal method can be used on single canvas, but uses slightly more thread than half cross stitch.

1 Starting at top right of the canvas, bring the needle out and up to the right, over one intersection. Insert it through the canvas, down under two horizontal threads and out to the front, and repeat to the end of the row.

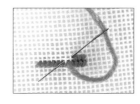

2 Next, turn the work upside down and work all subsequent rows in the same way.

BASKETWEAVE STITCH
This diagonal way of working produces a stronger stitch which does not distort the canvas as much as the horizontal methods, but does tend to use more wool.

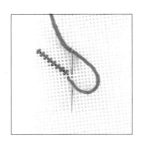

1 Work the first row from left to right. Pull the needle through taking it up to the right, over one intersection; bring it back to the front, from under two horizontal threads.

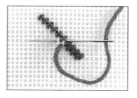

2 Work the return row upwards from right to left, inserting the stitches in the spaces left from the first row.

Diagonal Stitches

O ver the years many different needlepoint stitches have evolved and entire stitch dictionaries have been devoted to explaining them. They can be broken down, however, into just a few basic groups: those worked diagonally, with horizontal or vertical lines, and variations on cross stitch and star stitches. The diagonal stitches are useful background or filling stitches, ideal for covering large areas. They can be sewn in a single colour to give a smooth brocade-like surface, or in stripes for a more dramatic effect. The method of working means that there is a diagonal pull on the canvas, so the finished piece tends to become distorted.

From top to bottom: Moorish, Jacquard and Byzantine stitch.

BYZANTINE STITCH

This consists of diagonal zigzag rows, which can be worked over two, three or four intersections of the canvas. The size of each "step" can be varied, but should remain constant within the piece.

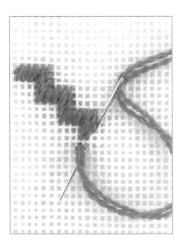

Work four diagonal stitches over two intersections, from left to right, then four stitches downwards. Repeat to form the zigzag, then work the subsequent rows in parallel. Fill in any space with graduated diagonal stitches.

JACQUARD STITCH

This is made up of two repeated zigzags. The basic stepped row of Byzantine stitch is worked over two intersections and followed by a row of tent stitch.

Stitch the first stepped row as before, then work the second line in diagonal stitches over one intersection, across, and then down the canvas.

MOORISH STITCH

Here the square elements of cushion (pillow) stitch are combined with zigzag lines. If Moorish stitch is worked in two colours, it produces a geometric checked pattern.

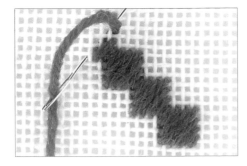

1 The first row consists of diagonal stitches worked over one, two, three, four, then three, two and one intersections.

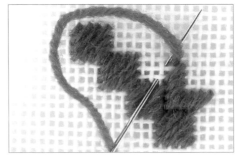

2 Work a line of stepped stitches over two intersections to fit alongside the first row and repeat these two rows.

From left to right: small diagonal mosaic stitch, condensed Scottish stitch and Milanese stitch.

SMALL DIAGONAL MOSAIC STITCH

Also known as Parisian stitch, this is made by following a tent stitch over one intersection with a longer stitch over two intersections. Work the sequence along a diagonal of the canvas, and work the next row so that it fits beside the first. It can be worked from right to left or left to right.

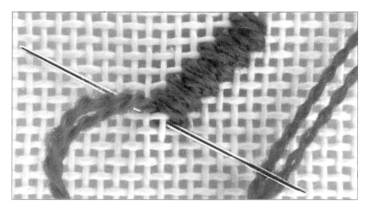

MILANESE STITCH

Diagonal rows of triangles facing in opposite directions make up this stitch, and it is particularly effective when worked in two colours.

CONDENSED SCOTTISH STITCH

This resembles parallel lines of interlocked diamond shapes and gives a strong diagonal appearance.

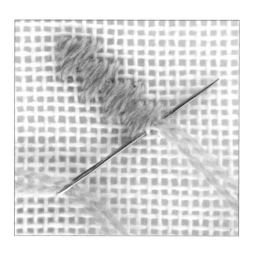

1 Work diagonal stitches over one, two, three and four intersections to form a triangle, then repeat the unit.

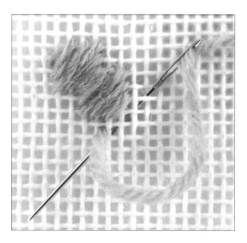

1 Work a unit of graduated stitches over two, three, four, and then three intersections. Repeat this along the diagonal.

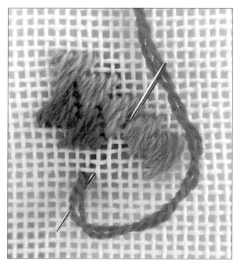

2 The second row is reversed, so that the shortest stitch fits next to the longest stitch of the first row.

2 Work the same sequence for the next row, interlocking the two lines so that the shortest stitch of one row fits against the longest. stitch of the adjacent row.

Square Stitches

This category includes diagonal, upright and horizontal elements, creating repeated square units, a chequerboard effect, and interesting variations when using more than one colour.

SMALL CUSHION (PILLOW) STITCH

Also known as mosaic stitch. When worked in a single colour, as in the finished sample, it gives an overall texture. Several colours produce a quite different effect.

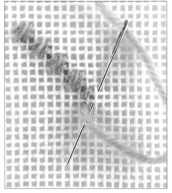

1 Start at the upper left and work diagonally downwards over first one, then two, intersections.

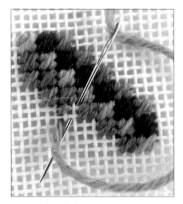

2 The following rows are worked up, then back down, so that each line fits into the previous stitches.

SCOTTISH STITCH

This gives a plaid effect, reminiscent of simple tartan patterns, which looks very effective when worked in contrasting yarns.

1 Work the grid first, using horizontal and vertical rows of tent stitch with a three- or four-thread space left between them.

2 Fill in the spaces with individual cushion (pillow) stitches.

From left to right: cushion (pillow) stitch, small cushion (pillow) stitch and Scottish stitch.

CUSHION (PILLOW) STITCH

This can be worked so that all the squares lie in the same direction, or at an angle to each other, which reduces the tension on the canvas.

1 This basic square is made up from seven stitches over one, two, three, four, three, two, then one intersections, worked in diagonal rows. For two-colour work, leave four thread spaces between rows.

2 Diagonal rows of the second colour are used to fill in the spaces.

CHEQUER (CHECKER) STITCH

This alternates small squares of tent stitch with lines of graduated diagonal stitch to produce an interesting texture, particularly when two colours are used.

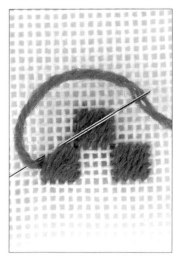

1 Work diagonal lines of cushion (pillow) stitch squares over four threads.

2 With the second colour, work four rows of four tent stitches to fill in the spaces.

BRIGHTON STITCH

This is worked in alternate rows of diagonal stitches which form a diamond pattern. The small spaces are filled in with upright cross stitch.

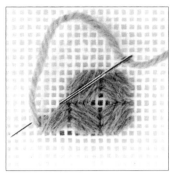

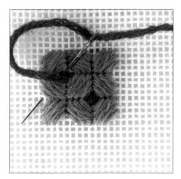

1 Start with a block of five diagonal stitches worked from left to right, then a second block slanting the other way. Work the next row so that it is a mirror image of the first.

2 Work an upright cross stitch, in the same or in a contrasting colour, over the two threads which have been left unworked between the stitches.

WOVEN STITCH

This stitch produces an intriguing basketweave effect, which appears to have been interwoven. It can also be worked in just one colour.

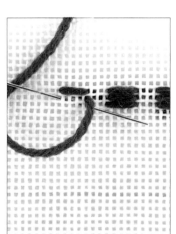

1 Working from right to left, make blocks of three parallel straight stitches over four threads, leaving a three- or four-thread space between. Work the next row so that the blocks lie immediately below the spaces above.

2 The second colour is used to fill in the spaces. Starting from the top right, work blocks of upright straight stitches over four threads, so that the first and last stitches of each block overlap the horizontal stitches from the first row.

From left to right: woven stitch, Brighton stitch and chequer (checker) stitch.

Crossed Stitches

T he foundation of this group is the simple
cross stitch, which is made from two
diagonal stitches crossing in the centre. Other
variations may combine upright and horizontal
stitches, and consist of repeated units of two or
four stitches. Crossed stitches should always be
sewn in the same order, so that the upper
stitches lie in the same direction.

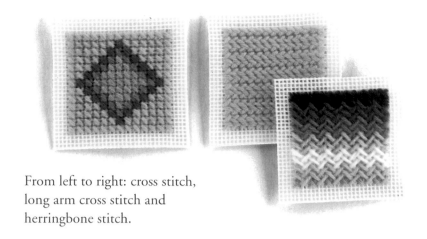

From left to right: cross stitch,
long arm cross stitch and
herringbone stitch.

CROSS STITCH

This can be worked singly, or in rows when larger areas need
to be covered. When small stitches, covering a single
intersection, are required, they should be worked on a
double or interlock canvas.

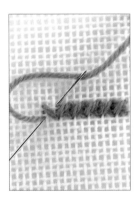

1 Individual cross stitches are
worked from right to left, then
from left to right. Bring out the
needle and take it up to the left over
two intersections. Push through the
canvas, pass down behind two
threads and bring it up. Work the
second stitch over the first and bring
the needle back to the starting point
of the second stitch.

2 When working in rows, make
the crosses in two passes. Form
the lower stitches by sewing from
right to left. Bring the needle out and
up to the left over two intersections,
and under two horizontal threads.
Repeat to the end.

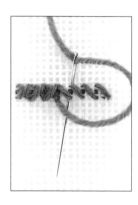

3 For the upper stitches, work a
line of separate diagonal
stitches in the same way, reversing
the direction so that they cover the
first line.

LONG ARM CROSS STITCH

Also known as Greek stitch, the long arm cross stitch forms a
braid-like line, made by the stitches crossing off centre. It
can be used singly as a border or in rows for a solid texture.

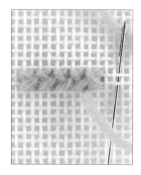

Work from left to right. Bring the
needle up over two threads and four
threads to the right to make a long
diagonal stitch. Insert under two
horizontal threads and bring up. Take
up to the left, over two intersections,
then insert under two horizontal
threads and bring up. Repeat both
stitches to the end of the row.

HERRINGBONE STITCH

This produces a dense woven look, particularly effective
when worked in stripes of tonal colours.

1 Starting at the upper left and
working from left to right, bring
the needle out and down diagonally
to the right over four intersections.
Pass left under two threads, then up
diagonally right over four
intersections. Pass the needle left
under two vertical threads and bring
out. Repeat to the end.

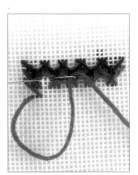

2 Start the next row and
subsequent rows two thread
spaces below the first stitch. Work
the stitch as before, so that the rows
interlock.

OBLONG STITCH VARIATION

This is made up of rows of longer stitches, which are held in place with small back stitches.

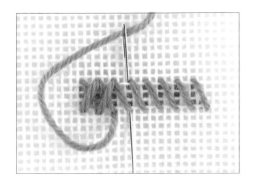

1 The base row is worked as for normal cross stitch, but the stitches are formed over four horizontal and two vertical threads.

2 Using a matching or contrasting thread, make a row of back stitches over the two vertical threads in the centre of each stitch.

DOUBLE STRAIGHT CROSS STITCH

This forms a raised diamond consisting of four separate stitches (two crosses). Each unit is worked separately and the same order of construction must always be followed to give a regular appearance.

1 Bring the needle up and over four horizontal threads. Pass behind under two intersections, out and over four vertical threads to form a large cross. Bring up at the left, through the space that lies between the two arms.

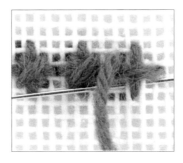

2 Form a second cross by taking the needle down over two intersections, behind and to the left under two vertical threads, then up to the right over two intersections.

RICE STITCH

This very attractive stitch covers the canvas completely. Each stitch unit consists of a cross stitch which is held down at each corner with a grain-like back stitch.

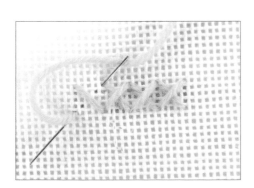

1 Work rows of large cross stitches over four intersections.

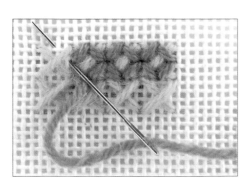

2 Using a contrasting colour, make four back stitches in a diamond shape over each cross.

From top to bottom: oblong stitch variation, double straight cross stitch, and rice stitch.

Star Stitches

Stars combine diagonal and straight lines to produce bold dramatic shapes which look particularly effective when worked in rows of complementary colours. They are used to create definite shapes and patterns, rather than to fill in backgrounds or large areas.

From top to bottom: ray stitch, Algerian eye stitch and Rhodes stitch.

ALGERIAN EYE STITCH

Made up of 16 stitches radiating from a centre point, this should be worked in a thickish thread with a fairly loose tension, so that the canvas is covered.

1 Each stitch is worked over four threads. Bring the needle up at the centre, then insert it to the left over four threads, and pull back up through the original space. Count two threads down and four across for the second stitch. Make the third stitch over four intersections down to the left, the fourth over four horizontal threads and two vertical ones. Continue, working counter-clockwise, until the whole square has been covered.

2 Further stitches can be worked in horizontal or vertical rows. Lines of back stitch, over two threads, surround the finished stitches.

RAY STITCH

Also known as fan stitch, this consists of five stitches and resembles one corner of Algerian eye stitch. Its lively appearance comes from working each row in opposite directions.

Bring the needle through and take it down over four threads, then back to the starting point. Count down four threads and two threads to the left for the second stitch, then work the third stitch over four intersections to the left. Count up two for the fourth stitch, and work back over four threads, then work the final stitch at right angles to the first.

RHODES STITCH

This is usually worked on a single canvas to produce a raised, highly textured surface. All the stitches are worked in the same direction so that they match.

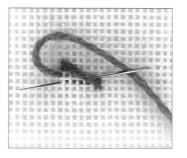

1 Bring the thread through, then count six threads to the right and four down. Insert the needle and bring back up one hole below the starting point and insert again, one hole above the end of the first stitch.

2 Continue working counter-clockwise in this way, until the whole six-thread square has been covered.

Straight Stitches

Straight stitches lie parallel with the weave and are usually worked on a single canvas so that the threads are covered completely. The most interesting variation is Florentine or flame stitch, used for Bargello work. This historic technique has long been popular, particularly in Italy. It is worked in repeated rows of an elaborate zigzag, and there are many variations on the basic pattern.

CHEVRON STITCH

This gives a strong horizontal zigzag pattern. Work over three to five threads to give wider or narrower bands.

1 Over four threads, work four straight lines, starting each stitch one hole up to the right, then work three stitches sloping downwards. Continue to the end of the row.

2 Work the second row in the same way, so that the chevrons fit neatly together.

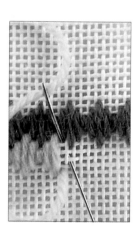

HUNGARIAN DIAMOND STITCH

A good filling stitch that can be worked in a single colour. The height of the stitches may be varied. Work a diamond shape of vertical stitches over two, four, six and four horizontal threads. Repeat to the end of the row. Work the next rows in the same way, with the longest stitch below the shortest stitch of the previous row.

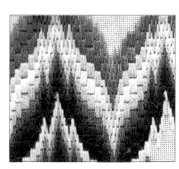

FLORENTINE STITCH

This is quick to work: once the first line has been stitched, the subsequent rows repeat the same series of peaks and valleys. Shades of the same colour can be used to give an antique feel to the work.

UPRIGHT GOBELIN STITCH

This resembles the ridged surface of hand-woven tapestries and is named after the work produced by the Gobelin family's factory in Paris.

Work from right to left, then from left to right. Bring the needle through, pass it down over two, three or four horizontal threads, then back up to form the next stitch.

GOBELIN FILLING STITCH

This can be used to produce subtle shaded effects, and can be worked in different lengths. The overlapping rows give a smooth surface.

Work a row of vertical stitches over six horizontal threads, leaving one row of holes between them. Work the next row between these stitches, starting three threads down from the top of the preceding row.

Clockwise from top: chevron stitch, Hungarian diamond stitch, Gobelin filling stitch and upright Gobelin stitch.

Patchwork and Quilting

Patchwork is constructed from shaped pieces of contrasting fabric, which are sewn together in geometric patterns to form a mosaic of cloth. Quilting is the process by which two sheets of fabric, with padding between them, are joined by lines of stitching. The top layer is often made from patchwork and so the two crafts are closely linked.

The word "quilt" comes from *culcita*, the Latin for a stuffed mattress or cushion (pillow); indeed, a thick bedcover, filled with yarn or even straw, was an essential domestic item in the days before effective heating. The earliest quilts were purely functional, but as time passed, they became more ornate.

Right: This nineteenth-century English quilt is made from dressmaker's remnants. The printed trompe-l'oeil fabric border gives the impression of a hexagonal patchwork.

Below: Patchwork looks effective on any scale. This small heart-shaped pincushion is made from fragments of antique cloth saved from an irreparably damaged quilt.

Quilting itself dates back as far as the Middle Ages, when protective padded garments were worn under armour. It was used for insulated doublets, petticoats and nightcaps, as well as for bedcovers. In the past, quilting was practised throughout Europe and was at its most popular in Britain, particularly in Wales and Northumbria. Distinctive wholecloth bedcovers, made from plain red or white woven cotton, were unique to these areas. The flowing quilted designs incorporated spirals, interlocking circles, hearts, feathers, waves and other natural imagery. In west Wales, children were sent out to collect leaves and petals from the hedgerows to use as templates. Making a quilt was part of the daily routine and often a family affair, with even the youngest members threading needles. Women did most of the sewing, and men cut the quilting templates from thin wood or tin.

The early pioneers from Britain and

Contemporary patchwork can be bold and graphic in design, like these velvet cushion (pillow) covers.

bees" were an important social event, usually held before haymaking, when friends and neighbours would gather together at dawn with the object of completing their work before sundown.

Quilters have always been resourceful and open to ideas. The first bedcovers were stitched and quilted by hand, but new techniques were eagerly adopted when domestic sewing machines appeared in the 1870s. Very often the patchwork would be pieced by machine, then the quilting designs worked by hand. This combination is

The Netherlands took basic household linens with them to America, but the comparative scarcity and high cost of cloth encouraged a new economy. Patchwork quilt tops used scraps salvaged from outworn clothing, while old blankets, rags or raw cotton were all used as fillings. In more remote areas, homespun cotton fabric was often used, coloured with the same vegetable dyes that the Native Americans used.

As more printed and patterned fabrics became available, the characteristic pattern blocks developed, based on a combination of squares, triangles and diamonds. Their names are a social document in themselves. They might reflect the makers' religious beliefs, as in "Star of Bethlehem" and "Garden of Eden", or the dangers of frontier

existence: "Bear's Paw", "Rocky Road to Kansas" and "Indian Hatchet". Some were named after individuals, such as "Aunt Sukey's Choice", and "Grandmother's Favourite", while others evoked the objects of everyday life: "Weather Vane", "Monkey Wrench" and "Churn Dash".

Tradition has it that a young woman had to make eleven bedcovers before she married, and that the twelfth was a rich wedding quilt. The pattern chosen for this would often contain visual references to the couple – a fragment of a flag for a soldier, nautical patterns for a sailor or the "Little School House" design for a teacher.

Patchwork tops were generally pieced by just one worker, but quilting was a community effort, with several women sewing around the frame. "Quilting

Pieces cut from furnishing fabrics and an embroidered traycloth have been combined to make this brightly coloured floral panel.

still used, but machine quilting is increasingly popular because it is so quick. Lightweight polyester waddings (battings) have superseded the old fillings and these can easily be quilted by machine. Specialist suppliers now stock the materials needed to make professionally finished quilts and new ways of transferring designs and shaped pieces have been introduced. Interest in these adaptable and creative needlecrafts is widespread and growing – they are a developing art and a living tradition.

Album quilts can be made as a group project, with each contributor making one block, or as a showcase for the many named traditional patterns.

Patchwork and Quilting
Tools and Materials

Only the most basic needlework tools are needed to start patchwork and quilting, although a range of equipment is now available to make precision cutting and assembly both easier and quicker. A sewing machine is useful for piecing techniques and a good steam iron is needed to prepare fabric and press seams.

FABRIC
The various materials used in a single project should all be of the same weight; medium-weight homespun checks, dressmaking cottons or lawn with small-scale designs are ideal, but should be washed before use to pre-shrink and remove any excess dye. Specialist mail-order companies stock a wide range of patchwork fabrics in both prints and complementary plain colours. Wadding (batting) for quilting is produced in both iron-on and sew-in variations in several weights. The old cotton type is still used today.

THREADS
Ordinary sewing thread is used for machine piecing and can be strengthened by running it over beeswax when quilting or hand sewing. Extra-strong quilting thread is available in a variety of colours.

TOOLS AND ACCESSORIES
Transparent rulers and square measures can be used to draw up templates or in conjunction with a rotary cutter to produce accurate fabric shapes. A cutting board will protect the work surface from the sharp blade of the cutter. Dressmaker's shears should have sharp blades and be kept only for cutting fabric; use another pair for paper or card and small embroidery scissors for cutting threads. Ready-made templates come in geometric shapes with clear plastic windows. Dressmaker's chalk or special quilter's pencils can be used to mark seam allowances or quilting patterns on to fabric and fine rust-proof dressmaker's pins are used to hold the pieces together. Short quilter's needles are best for hand quilting and a metal thimble provides very necessary protection. Special quilter's thimbles and finger guards are also produced.

Quilting threads.

Sewing cotton.

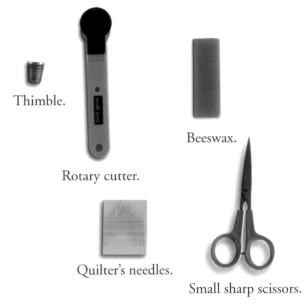

Thimble.

Rotary cutter.

Beeswax.

Quilter's needles.

Small sharp scissors.

Quilting hoop.

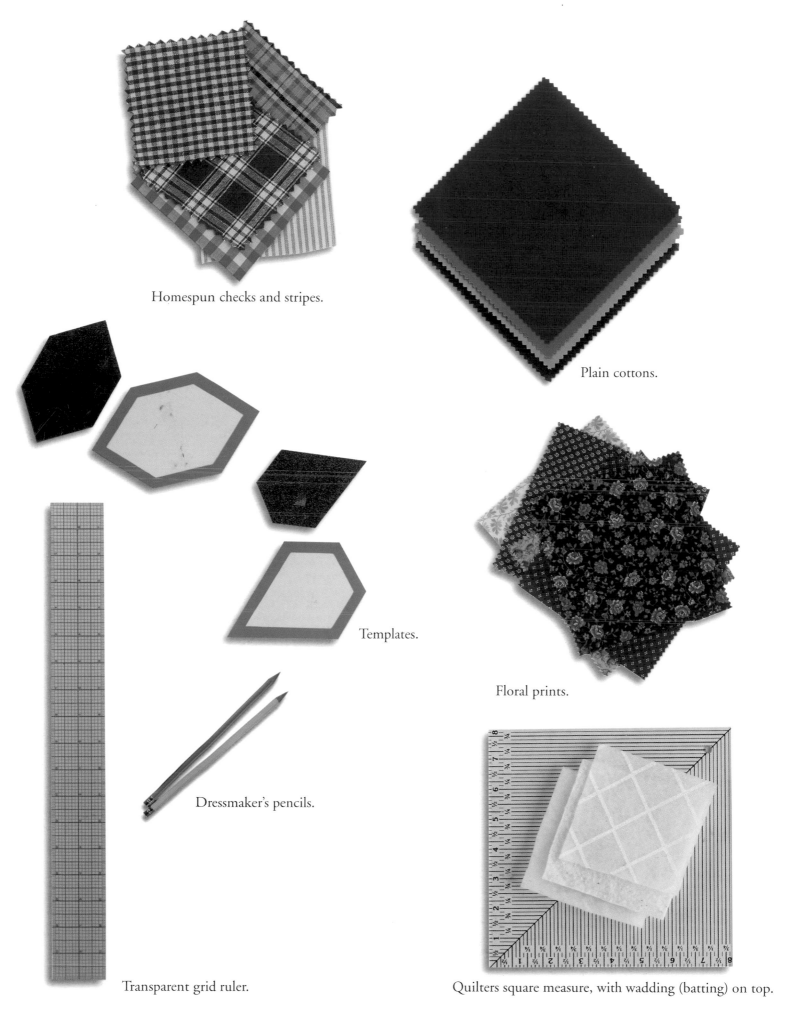

Homespun checks and stripes.

Plain cottons.

Templates.

Floral prints.

Dressmaker's pencils.

Transparent grid ruler.

Quilters square measure, with wadding (batting) on top.

49

Cutting Out and Piecing

There are three ways of piecing or joining patchwork pieces: by machine, by hand or with backing papers. Machining is quickest, but hand sewing gives a traditional, slightly irregular seam. For the beginner, working over backing papers is the best way to make precise diamonds and other angled shapes. Whichever method is chosen, meticulous measurement and cutting, careful stitching and thorough pressing are all vital for a professional finish.

Right: The checkerboard centre of this cushion (pillow) cover was cut from striped seersucker and remnants of floral furnishing fabric.

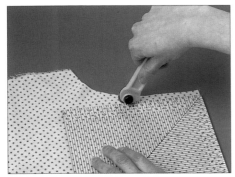

1 USING A ROTARY CUTTER
Working on a cutting mat, match one corner of the measure to the grain of the fabric. Keeping the cutter upright, run it firmly along the measure, and cut along the two sides.

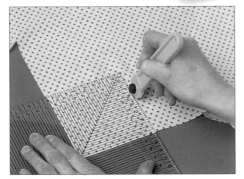

2 Turn the measure and line up the markings with the two cut edges to form the size of square required. Cut around the other two sides.

3 Squares can be cut in half diagonally to form triangles. Strips and rectangles can be cut using a transparent ruler marked with a grid.

1 MACHINE PIECING SQUARES Set the machine to straight stitch and adjust to 10 stitches every 2.5cm (1in). Pin or hold two squares together, right sides facing and sew along one edge. Leave a seam allowance of 6mm (¼in), using the lines on the machine bed as a guide. Several pairs can be sewn in a continuous line, then cut apart.

2 Join the pairs into strips, then press the seam allowances to one side. Sew the strips together, matching the joins, so that the allowances lie in opposite directions.

1 HAND
PIECING
To be sure of a
neat seam, the
allowance –
usually 6mm
(¼in) – is marked
on the back of
the fabric. With
window templates,
the metal shape can be used as a guide, or rule a line with a
quilter's pencil or fading pen.

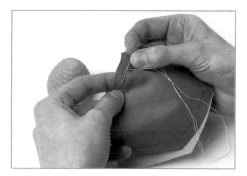

2 Cut a length
of sewing
thread, about
45cm (18in)
long, and
strengthen by
pulling it against
a beeswax block.
Knot the end,
then, holding the two pieces right sides together, make a
line of small tidy running stitches along the edge. Finish
with a back stitch.

1 WORKING WITH BACKING
PAPERS Special templates with a
transparent plastic window are useful
when using patterned fabrics, but they
must be lined up with the grain. The
dark edge represents the seam allowance.

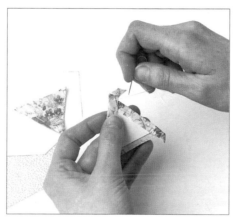

2 Use the metal shape as a guide for
cutting the backing paper. Pin or
tack (baste) it to the centre of the fabric
shape, then fold the seam allowance
over the paper and tack (baste) down,
one side at a time.

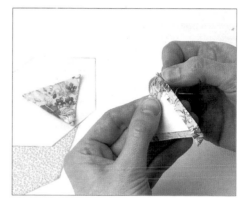

3 When working over sharp angles,
the surplus fabric can be mitred to
a neat point and tacked (basted) down.
The pieces are joined together with
over-stitching (see method for
hexagons); the tacking (basting) stitch
and papers are then removed.

This mosaic is
based on a tile
design from the
Alhambra in
Spain. The
interlocking
shapes were
worked over
papers to achieve
a flat and accurate
pattern.

Storm at Sea

T his stunning pattern originated on the eastern seaboard of the United States. The overall effect is one of lively flowing movement, suggesting ocean waves, but all the seams are, in fact, straight. Although complex at first sight, the patchwork is made up of just three different blocks: the large pale blue square is bordered on each side by a blue diamond block, with small dark blue squares at each corner. The method for making these is also a general guide to machine piecing techniques for triangles. To construct the actual pattern, draw up a set of templates on squared paper using the finished picture as a guide.

1 The large and small square blocks are pieced in the same way. Sew a white triangle to each side of the smallest square, stitching 6mm (¼in) from the edge. Press the seams so that the allowance faces inwards.

2 Sew a blue triangle along each edge of the square, carefully pinning to match the seams. It may be helpful to tack (baste) the pieces together first.

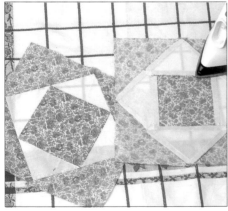

3 The large square blocks are pieced in the same order. Press the allowance out towards the corners. This prevents the fabric showing through the white cotton.

4 The diamond-shaped blocks are constructed from two squares, each consisting of a dark triangle with a narrow white triangle stitched to two sides.

5 Lay the completed blocks out in rows and stitch together. Careful pinning and tacking (basting) is necessary when working with such large pieces, to keep the seams and joins regular.

Bear's Paw

Bear's paw or bear's track is an early American pattern, supposedly inspired by pawprints left in the mud. It is a repeating design with the square blocks joined with bands of fabric or sashing. In the past, a patchwork quilt top was worked in one piece, then quilted on a large frame, but today there is not always time or room to do this. Instead, the blocks can be quilted individually, then joined.

Above: This bear's paw quilt has been made entirely from recycled fabric such as old gingham shirts and white sheeting.

1 Each block is made up of four "paws" surrounding a small square and with a row of three white squares between them. Follow the main picture to assemble the block.

2 Cut pieces of backing fabric and wadding (batting) slightly larger than the finished block and tack (baste) together, working from the centre out. Be sure that the layers lie flat. Quilt along the seam lines. To join the completed blocks, stitch them together in strips, divided by bands of single white squares.

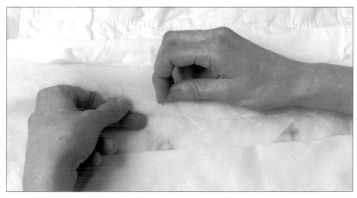

3 When joining the blocks, sew through the top layer only and press seam flat. Trim the excess wadding (batting) so the edges just touch. Sew the wadding with a loose flat stitch.

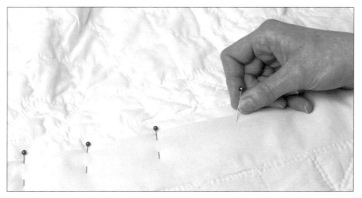

4 To neaten the back seams, fold and sew each seam so it overlaps onto the next square. Slip stitch then complete the quilting along the remaining seam lines.

Hexagonal Patchwork

U nlike block designs, which may consist of many different-shaped pieces, hexagonal patchwork uses just one shape. The pattern is formed by the choice and arrangement of colours within the honeycomb grid made by the interlocking repeat. Hexagons are traditionally worked over backing papers, which should be firm enough to hold their shape but not so thick that they are difficult to sew through. A quicker way of piecing is to use a lightweight washable interfacing. This remains inside the patches, giving them extra support.

1 JOINING HEXAGONS Use a template as a guide for cutting papers or, if interfacing is being used, draw on to it directly with a sharp pencil, then cut out.

Above: Silks and velvets were used to make this antique-effect cushion (pillow) cover; the use of a black outline around the rosettes is particularly dramatic.

2 Iron the interfacing to the wrong side of the fabric following the manufacturer's instructions and keeping the shapes parallel to the grain. Cut out, leaving a margin of at least 6mm (¼in) all around.

4 The patches are joined with a neat stitch, which should pass through the fabric without picking up any of the interfacing. Hold the pieces together with right sides facing.

3 Turn the seam allowance back over the iron-on interfacing. Take care not to crease the hexagon. Finally, tack (baste) down all around using small stitches.

5 Six coloured patches can be sewn around a contrasting centre to make a rosette. These are then joined to make an all-over pattern. Take out the tacking (basting) when the work is complete.

Patchwork Gallery

The heritage of patchwork patterns is enormous; there are literally hundreds of named designs and variations from which to choose, and all quiltmakers bring their own individual interpretation to their work.

Geometric patterns, sometimes from surprising sources, can be adapted – the scope is limitless. The selection on this page illustrates what is possible, both for the beginner and for the more experienced worker.

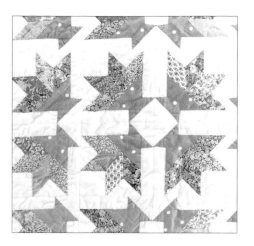

Left: "Basket of scraps" consists of four patterned diamonds set on a triangle. It makes a good showcase for different floral prints. The blocks could also be set in rows all facing the same way.

Above: "Dresden plate" originated in the United States in the 1920s. It is a combination of appliquéd and patchwork techniques which looks most effective when fabrics of a similar pattern density are used together.

Left: "Ships in harbour" shows how a complicated pattern can be built up by repeating a simple square block. Study the design carefully to see how this is done.

Left: This abstract patchwork is made up from randomly arranged plain and patterned squares and uses fragments of hand-dyed cotton and satin.

Above: A drawing of a Roman pavement was the basis for this example, which is made up of squares and long hexagonal shapes. The use of a strong plain colour against a subtly patterned background gives depth to the design.

Left: This intricate *trompe-l'oeil* design, a variation of "tumbling blocks", was worked over backing papers. The basic unit is a 3-D hexagon surrounded by nine diamonds.

Crazy Patchwork

There was a great vogue for this highly ornamental patchwork in the late nineteenth century; it appealed to the Victorians' desire for lavish interior decoration and their love of thrift, as even the smallest and most irregular scraps of fabric can be incorporated. It is worked in individual squares which can be used singly, or joined to make a throw or quilt.

1 Collect together remnants of silk, velvet, brocade and furnishing fabric. Cut out and arrange random pieces of material into a square, then cut a square of calico (cotton lining fabric) to use as the foundation.

2 The patches can be hand sewn on to the calico (lining fabric) with running stitch, or machined with a matching or contrasting decorative stitch. Work from one edge across the square, attaching one piece at a time.

3 Embroidered or appliquéd motifs can be added for a luxurious effect.

Above: This fringed cushion (pillow) incorporates fragments of Indian woven braid with silk salvaged from old ties. It has been embroidered with a variety of elaborate stitches.

4 Further decoration can be added by disguising the seams with embroidery stitches worked in bright colours. Feather stitch and its variations are especially popular.

Somerset Patchwork

Somerset and crazy patchwork both involve stitching individual pieces of material on to a foundation fabric, instead of piecing them together. Neither technique is really suitable for items that will get a lot of wear and tear, but both are attractive and intriguing to construct. For the best result, choose strong, contrasting colours to form the folded star design. Dressmaking-weight cottons will give a crisp edge and are not too bulky, as the finished piece is made up of many layers.

Above: Craft fabric in small-scale prints was used to make this festive Christmas decoration.

1 Each triangle is made from a rectangle, with its length twice the width, plus 6mm (¼in) seam allowance at one long edge. Press under the turning, then fold the neatened edges over to make a right-angled triangle.

2 Cut a square of firm cotton. Fold and press diagonally each way from corner to corner, then in half vertically and horizontally. Arrange the first four triangles as shown, and sew in place along the outer edges. Sew each point with a small invisible stitch.

3 The next eight triangles are arranged to match up with the guides, so that a star shape is created. Measure each piece before stitching, so that they are all equidistant.

4 Continue to build up the pattern in contrasting rounds, making sure that each layer overlaps the previous one.

WORKING IN THE ROUND This technique can also be worked over a large polystyrene ball. Work in two halves, pin the triangles in place and cover the join with a ribbon.

Suffolk Puffs (Yo-yo Patchwork)

Suffolk puff, also known as yo-yo patchwork, has a charming flower-like appearance. It is quick to assemble from gathered circles of fabric, which can be lightly padded to give extra depth. Different patterns can be created by arranging the yo-yos in stripes or concentric circles. The finished piece drapes well and makes an attractive bedcover, especially if placed over a coloured blanket which shows through the gaps. Alternatively, it can be made more hardwearing by backing with a contrasting fabric.

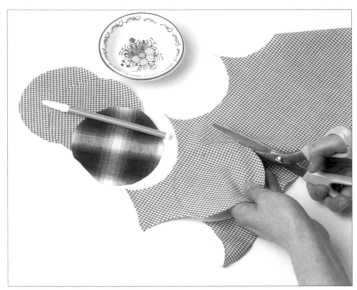

1 Cut a circle of card measuring between 7.5cm (3in) and 15cm (6in), or use a suitable saucer as a template. With this as a guide, cut out the patches, grouping them according to colour. Light cotton fabrics, fine enough to gather without being bulky, are best.

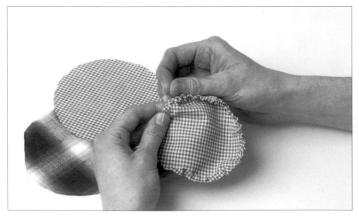

2 Turn under a narrow hem to the wrong side of the fabric around the edge of the circle. Stitch down with small running stitches, using a strong thread.

Above: The circles can be joined in rows, as shown in the steps, but a denser effect can be achieved by setting them in a honeycomb arrangement to form hexagonal shapes.

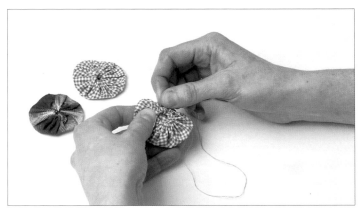

3 Carefully pull up the thread and distribute the folds evenly. Be sure that all the raw edges lie on the inside. Secure with a few back stitches and trim the thread.

4 When all the circles have been prepared, sort them into groups of colour and lay them out on the finished design. Join the edges where they touch with several strong stitches, without distorting the shape.

Cathedral Window

Cathedral window, like Suffolk puff (yo-yo Patchwork), is a fascinating technique which does not need to be lined or quilted. The distinctive lattice is formed by joining folded squares of plain fabric to frame small patches of patterned material. It is important to cut and stitch accurately to achieve a uniform result.

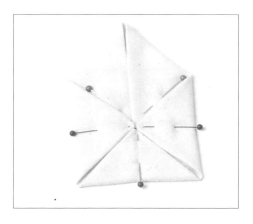

1 Cut a square of cotton or calico twice the size of the finished square, plus a hem of 6mm (¼in). Press under the allowance along each side.

Above: This dramatic example uses metallic fabrics to give a jewel-like effect. It combines Cathedral Window patchwork with a variation known as Secret Garden.

2 Fold the four corners to the middle of the square so that the points meet exactly and press. Pin in place.

4 Sew the cotton squares together, right sides facing, to form a block. The coloured patches are fixed on to the diamonds created between the sewn-together squares.

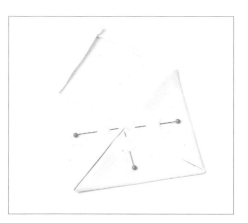

3 Fold the double thickness corners to the centre, press the creases and pin in place. Sew the four points firmly and neatly together with a matching thread.

5 Cut a square of fabric 6mm (¼ in) smaller than the diamond and pin in place. Fold the sides of the four surrounding squares back over the raw edges of the fabric and stitch down. Triangles can be used to fill in the spaces at the sides.

Hand and Machine Quilting

Quilting simply involves working lines of hand or machine stitching to hold a padded filling between two pieces of fabric. The stitches pass through all three layers. It is often used to enhance a piece of patchwork, but is also an independent technique; designs worked on to plain fabrics are known as wholecloth motifs. There are many traditional variations, often based on natural imagery. Quilting patterns can be transferred by the methods used for embroidery, but cardboard templates are often used for repeated shapes.

1 HAND QUILTING Place the template on to the fabric and draw round the edge with a dressmaker's fading pen.

Above: Quilting stitches can be used in a free and illustrative way. This padded cherub was painted on to silk and outlined with back stitch.

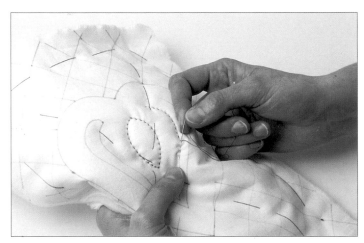

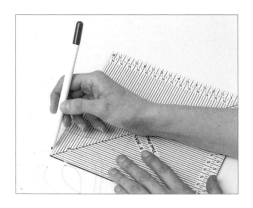

2 Use a graded measure to rule the parallel lines that form the characteristic grid pattern. Be sure that they are set at right angles.

4 Using strong quilting thread, sew over the outline with a small running stitch. To avoid the knot showing on the back, tug the thread so that it is pulled through the fabric into the wadding (batting). Pick up three or four stitches at a time and stitch with an even motion.

3 Sandwich the wadding (batting) between the top cloth and a piece of backing fabric. Tack (baste) together diagonally and around the outside edge, so that the surface lies smoothly.

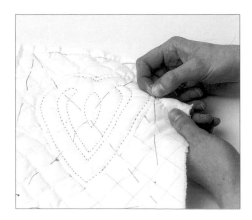

5 Do not carry loose threads across the back of the work, but sew each line of the design separately by passing the needle through the quilt. Finish off with a back stitch.

QUILTING ON PATCHWORK As well as serving the practical purpose of anchoring the wadding (batting), quilting can add depth and texture to a piece of patchwork. Here *(left)* it has been used to emphasize the eight diamonds that make up the "birds-in-the-air" design.
A line of stitching is worked either side of each seam.

TRANSFER TO DARK FABRICS Regular motifs such as this flower can be drawn using a template from which one repeating petal has been cut out.

Draw round the outline first, then move the template one step at a time and mark the curved lines.

Above: Quilting designs can be worked in light thread on a dark background for a strong visual contrast. A quilter's silver pencil will show up well and gives a fine line.

MACHINE QUILTING Quilting by machine gives a very regular appearance to the finished piece and is quick to do. Some sewing machines have special quilting attachments which are helpful when sewing in parallel rows. Be sure that the tension is adjusted correctly before starting and stitch slowly at a regular pace.

The layers must be well tacked (basted) so that they do not shift. Use a thread to match the fabric and stitch as close to the seam as possible. Both hands should guide the work under the presser foot.

61

Quilting Gallery

Over the years, quilting has been used to produce many decorative effects, in conjunction with patchwork or on its own. This collection of old and new examples shows just what can be achieved and should provide a great source of inspiration.

Above: The rows of stitching that quilt these antique bedcovers had to be worked closely to hold in place the rather unstable cotton filling.

Above: The hearts and interlaced knots on this machine-stitched wedding quilt are symbols of love and betrothal. It is a beautiful example of how a traditional design can be interpreted in a contemporary way.

Left: Instead of outlining the patchwork pieces, the maker of this turkey red bear's paw motif has quilted it with a grid of white stitching, worked across the entire surface.

Left: The handle of the green basket has been "echo" quilted, with the shape repeated in concentric lines, while the overlapping strips that make up the pineapple motif have been simply outlined.

Below: These entertaining hearts are made from padded and quilted velvet and trimmed with fake fur.

Above: Outline stitching has been used to define just the white triangles of this floral patchwork border. New types of polyester waddings (battings) do not have to be stitched as densely as the old cotton fillings.

3-Dimensional Quilting

PADDED QUILTING

A quick and effective way of giving a quilted look to a printed fabric is to pad individual motifs. This works well on floral chintzes and can be used for soft furnishings, to give interest to cushions (pillows) or headboards.

1 Tack (baste) the printed fabric together with a piece of thick wadding (batting) and a cotton backing cloth. Be sure the layers all lie flat.

2 Pick out a few flowers that are evenly spaced across the surface and sew around them, through all three layers, with either a straight or satin stitch, following the outline closely.

3 When complete, turn over and cut away the excess wadding (batting) between the stitched areas. For extra depth, make a slit in the backing fabric, stuff in a small amount of wadding (batting) and stitch back together.

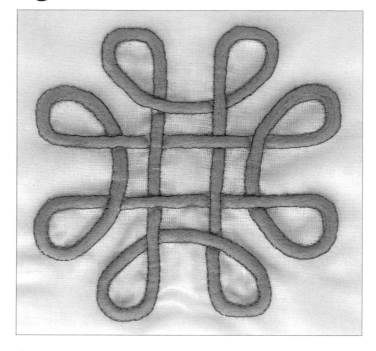

CORD QUILTING Interlaced patterns such as this Celtic knot can be created by threading a soft yarn or cord through a stitched channel. The shadow effect is created by using a sheer fabric for the top layer so that the green yarn shows through.

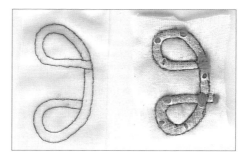

Outline the design with two evenly spaced rows of back stitch *(left)*. Working from the back, thread a tapestry needle with cord and insert between the lines of stitching. Bring the needle out and back to get round the curves, leaving a small loop so that it does not pull *(right)*.

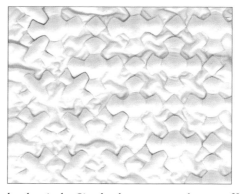

TRAPUNTO QUILTING This complex design was worked by tacking (basting) two layers of fabric together and outlining the design with back stitch. Single shapes were then stuffed with wadding (batting), as above. This padded technique can be used with cord quilting to create interesting effects.

Appliqué

Appliqué, or applied work, is the craft of creating a design by sewing cut-out shapes from one material on to a background cloth. Unlike patchwork, where pieces are joined to create a new fabric, appliquéd shapes are added to an existing foundation. Its origins were strictly utilitarian, arising from the need to repair damage, but appliqué has developed into an extravagant art form in itself.

Appliqué is, even so, inextricably linked to patchwork and quilting, and the three techniques often appear together. Cut-out shapes can be more ornamental than pieced work and detailed patterns can be created. Appliqué is often used to add detail to geometric motifs, or to create lavish swags to border a patchwork design.

In eighteenth-century Britain, appliqué was used to conserve fragments of fine fabric, and to produce new bedspreads and wall hangings. New and exotic textiles, such as the Indian tree of life designs, were valued as highly as porcelain and other imported artefacts, so every precious scrap had to be used. Wealthy ladies of leisure, living in grand houses, would cut out the printed motifs and

This bird design, in strong primary colours, comes from the Indian district of Barmer, near Pakistan. It is finished with chain stitch.

reassemble them on to a new backing. Many examples of their work have been preserved in their original locations, valued for the skill involved in making them and for the intrinsic worth of the fabric itself.

Distinctive appliqué techniques have evolved in many areas of the world, as part of the needlework traditions of diverse cultures. In the Indian state of Gujarat, appliqué is used in the home for cushions, bedspreads and door-hangings, while large-scale pattern-cut banners and canopies have ceremonial

significance. The motifs used are bright and bold, so that they have great visual impact in a bustling procession.

The clothing of the tribal people of the north of Thailand is adorned with panels of intricate reverse appliqué. Here colour plays as important a role as patterns, and younger women traditionally wear much brighter and more vibrantly coloured clothing than their elders.

Perhaps the most spectacular appliqué quilts are those originally made in Hawaii. The technique was introduced

Soft pastel cottons, edged with blanket stitch, are used in traditional floral Chinese appliqué. Other embroidery stitches are used to add detail.

show off skilled needlework. The Baltimore bride quilts were the most spectacular of these.

The Depression years of the 1930s meant a revival of the thrift element in appliqué, and new patterns developed. Earlier designs had been based on natural forms – wild roses, ferns, feathers and honeysuckles – but new, more urban forms began to be incorporated. Contemporary album quilts provide a fascinating record of day-to-day life, with silhouette cut-outs of such mundane objects as teapots, shoes, scissors, bottles and table-lamps. Inspiration also came from the outside world and current events. One quilt made in 1939, has a dramatic appliqué design of aircraft, to commemorate Lindbergh's transoceanic flight.

Appliqué has a fascinating international heritage which is not fixed in the past. New materials such as iron-on fusible bonding and interfacing means that a wide range of fabrics can now be used to create projects that will take this ancient craft into a new century.

Right: A variety of appliqué and embroidery techniques has been cleverly incorporated into this recreation of a child's drawing.

by missionaries, who provided the local people with cloth and thread. They brought with them the customs of American patchwork and appliqué, which use small pieces of fabric. The Hawaiian women, however, had no history of re-using scraps and so cut out large, quilt-sized motifs from single sheets of folded cloth. Their imagery was drawn from their island surroundings: grape vines, seaweed, coral, palms and luxurious tropical flowers in vibrant colours such as fuchsia, jade and deep sea green.

It is in America, however, that the most famous tradition grew up. The early settlers made quilts primarily to

keep warm as they moved westward. On the Eastern seaboard, as life became more stable, there was more time to sew. Complicated appliqué star, foliage and plume patterns evolved and appliqué became a virtuoso way to

Almost any fabric can be used for appliqué: a rough textured white towelling was chosen to make the body of this charming goose design.

Appliqué
Tools and Materials

Appliqué techniques are closely related to, and often combined with, patchwork and quilting, which means that essentially the same materials and tools are required for all three crafts.

FABRICS
In addition to the printed and patterned cottons used for patchwork, there are many unusual fabrics that can be used for applied decoration which would not be suitable for piecing. Metallic organzas (organdies), translucent sari fabrics, "Fortuny"-style pleated synthetics, velvets and textured weaves are all ideal for experimental work. Individual floral or geometric motifs can be cut from furnishing fabrics. Craft fabrics – printed with special designs for patchwork and appliqué – can be used to make personal Christmas or other gifts. Brightly coloured felts lend themselves naturally to this type of work, as they do not fray. Iron-on interfacing is useful to back and strengthen fabrics and iron-on fusible bonding is an effective way of attaching cut-out shapes to a background fabric.

THREADS
Sewing thread is used for tacking (basting) and for slip stitching down appliquéd shapes. Hand embroidery in a variety of threads can add interest and disguise raw edges, while machine satin stitch gives a tidy border. Striped or metallic threads are particularly effective.

TOOLS AND EQUIPMENT
Sharp fabric scissors with both long and short blades are necessary for accurate cutting of appliquéd shapes. Fine pins will hold work together before stitching – make sure they do not rust. Dressmaker's pens or chalk or carbon will be needed for transferring templates to fabric.

Iron-on interfacing.

Dressmaker's carbon.

Dressmaker's fading pen.

Dressmaker's pins.

Dressmaker's shears.

Needles.

Small sharp scissors.

Printed and woven cottons.

Felt.

Metallic and velvet fabrics.

Craft fabrics.

Machine embroidery threads.

Sewing thread.

Striped machine threads.

Embroidery threads.

Traditional Hand Techniques

The basic hand appliqué techniques have been used by generations of quilt-makers to produce a wealth of naturalistic and geometric patterns. These should be worked in closely woven fabrics of similar weight, such as percale or cotton lawn, which are easy to handle. It is important to match the grain of the cut-out motifs with that of the background to reduce stress on the fabric.

BASIC METHOD
Some workers use a quilting hoop to maintain an even tension across the background fabric, but this is a personal preference; if the pieces are pressed and tacked (basted) properly, and the stitching is even, there should be no risk of puckering. There are many pattern source books for those who want to recreate traditional designs. These are usually illustrated at actual size and a turning allowance of approximately 6mm (¼in) has to be added all round. Trace the template on to thin cardboard. Cut out and draw around it onto the fabric. Draw a second line 6mm (¼in) beyond this outline and cut around it. Fold the edge under, back to the inner line, and tack (baste). Clip the curves, if necessary, to reduce bulk. Tack (baste) on to the background fabric, then stitch down. Press and remove the tacking (basting) thread.

CURVED LINES
Thin lines such as those used for stems are cut on the bias so that they lie flat.

1 To make a stem 3mm (⅛in) wide, cut a 10mm (⅜in) strip of fine cotton fabric diagonally across the grain. Finger-press and tack (baste) down a narrow hem along each edge.

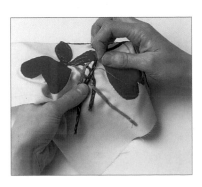

2 Bias strips are very flexible and can be interwoven to form intricate patterns as they are tacked (basted) into place.

Left: The strong curved shape of the serpent that encircles this contemporary Egyptian design has been emphasized with an outline of couched black thread, and fine detail has been added with back stitch.

CURVES AND CIRCLES
The curved sides of symmetrical shapes such as hearts and circles must be smooth and regular. One way to be sure of a professional finish is to press the cut-out shape over backing paper before sewing it down.

1 Cut out the shape, including the seam allowance. Cut a second template from paper, then tack (baste) the fabric over it, gathering slightly around the curves and clipping into the point at the inside corner.

2 Press from the wrong side with a hot iron.

3 Take out the tacking (basting) stitches and remove the backing paper. Tack (baste) the shape on to the backing fabric and stitch down. Make a few close stitches at the top of the heart to prevent fraying.

POINTS AND ANGLES

The surplus fabric at the outside corners should be mitred to give a neat finish.

1 Fold down the corner and trim the point.

2 Fold in the two adjacent sides and tack (baste) down, gathering slightly if they are curved.

Above: The raw edges of the fabric have also been used as a feature in this American flag, which makes good use of printed and woven cotton.

Above: Appliqué does not always have to obey the rules. The folk-art appeal of this bird relies upon the designer's deliberate disregard for formal technique. The shapes are cut from a sophisticated selection of matching checks, but sewn down with naive bold stitches.

STITCHING

The individual elements of the design should be tacked (basted) into place, then sewn down, using a matching sewing thread and small, almost invisible slip stitches. Working from right to left, knot the thread and bring the needle through the outside edge. Pick up a few threads of the adjacent backing fabric, then slip the needle through the folded edge for 3mm (⅛in). Bring the needle out and pull tight. Finish off securely and remove the tacking (basting).

Left: The order of assembling the separate elements should be planned carefully before starting, and it is helpful to number the pieces. The outside edges of the four segments that make up the inner circle of this design were sewn down last to conceal the raw ends of the stems.

Printed Fabric Appliqué

The idea of cutting motifs and pictures from printed fabrics and reassembling them to form a new decorative image is a very old one. In the eighteenth century it was known as Broderie Perse, after the elaborate floral chintzes and cretonnes that were imported from the East. Such materials were highly prized for their rarity so, for reasons of economy, individual birds, flowers and/or leaves were cut out from them.

These were then pasted on to a background fabric, in a new arrangement, and stitched in place, to make bedcovers or wallhangings.

This textile version of découpage is even easier to put into practice today; there is an enormous range of printed fabrics available, and new chemical solutions to prevent cut edges from fraying can be found in most craft shops and department stores.

1 Following the manufacturer's instructions, apply anti-fraying solution around the outline of the selected motif and allow to dry thoroughly.

2 Use a pair of sharp embroidery scissors to cut out the shape.

3 Sew on to the background fabric with a small neat stitch in matching thread. This collage technique is not really suitable for garments or items that might receive heavy wear, but is ideal for decorative panels or pictures.

4 It is possible to cut very fine details from treated fabric. This heavy furnishing satin is printed with an intricate paisley pattern.

An assortment of old and new fabrics, all printed with roses, was used to create this floral spray. These fabrics ranged from acetate headscarves of the 1950s and souvenir handkerchiefs, to a Provençale cotton print and contemporary dressmaking materials. Visual cohesion is given to the design by the careful selection of motifs from within a narrow colour range.

Lace Appliqué

A natural progression from using printed fabrics for appliqué is to cut out separate motifs from lace. Anti-fraying solutions are very effective when used on sheer and fine materials, and lace is particularly suitable. Choose machine-made lace with a design that has a clearly defined pattern. Guipure lace, with its strong floral designs, is ideal for this. Old and new lace can be mixed, and the subtle shades blend together well. This form of appliqué is the perfect way to utilize some of the odds and ends of trimmings that gather in every sewing box.

1 Collect scraps of lace, then apply a thin layer of anti-fraying solution to the edge of the most interesting motifs. The lace should not discolour, but it will become slightly stiffer to the touch.

2 Leave to dry, then cut out the individual motifs with sharp embroidery scissors.

Above: Reminiscent of a Victorian paper Valentine card, this pink satin heart is surrounded by lace motifs, appliquéd on to a background of floral cotton lawn. The inner circle is made up of fragments cut from a damaged length of antique lace, which has been washed to restore its original crisp white appearance.

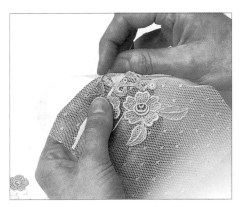

3 Sew the lace on to a backing using matching thread and small tidy stitches. A sheer or openweave fabric gives a light airy feel to the work. This technique could be used to make a romantic border for a bride's veil.

4 Try experimenting with different background fabrics, which can change the appearance of the work; here the net has been appliquéd on to toning satin, and seed pearls added.

In a different mood, these lace motifs have been stitched on to fine habutai silk and a cotton fabric, which has been screen- and transfer-printed with multi-layered images. They add texture and a feeling of nostalgia to the piece.

Using Fusible Bonding

Small motifs can be easily stitched on to a background fabric and will lie smoothly on the surface, but bigger shapes need to have extra support to keep them flat. Iron-on fusible bonding is an ideal way to fix two layers of fabric together. It consists of a soft web of heat-activated adhesive attached to greaseproof paper. The result is permanent, hard-wearing and washable – ideal for decorating garments or soft furnishings.

1 Select a motif from patterned fabric and cut out roughly.

2 Cut a piece of fusible bonding to size and iron firmly on to the back of the motif, with the paper side upwards, until the adhesive has melted.

This exuberant figure is appliquéd in plain cotton fabrics. The main pieces have been attached to the backing with fusible bonding and outlined with machine stitching. The details are hand-embroidered.

3 Allow to cool, then trim away the surplus fabric, cutting carefully around the outline. Peel away the backing paper.

4 Place the motif on the background material and iron according to the manufacturer's instructions. Press (do not slide) for about fifteen seconds with a hot dry iron.

Flying cherubs have been cut from Christmas craft fabric and bonded on to contrasting backgrounds to make these engaging greetings cards.

5 The raw edge of the motif will not fray now, but it can be neatened with a decorative line of machine satin stitch. Adjust the setting to a close zigzag and sew carefully, ensuring that the stitching is worked half on the motif and half on the backing fabric. A transparent foot, if supplied with the machine, makes it easier to guide the fabric. Pull the ends of thread through to the back and tie off.

Reverse Machine Appliqué

Reverse appliqué is an interesting variation on the basic technique. Instead of building up separate elements on a background material, the design is created by stitching several contrasting fabrics together and then parts of them are cut away to reveal underlying layers. There are long traditions of this branch of textile art around the world, many of which involve intricate hand stitching. Dramatic and effective results can, however, be achieved quickly by using a sewing machine.

Right: Different weights and textures of fabric have been mixed for this sunburst cushion (pillow). The soft pile of the velvet contrasts with the two shades of metallic organza (organdy) for a luxurious result. The width of the zigzag has been varied to emphasize the design, and a feeling of depth is given by stitching with both dark and light threads.

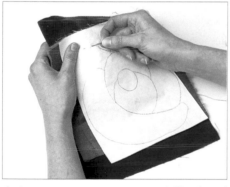

1 Select a design – bold graphic shapes are best – and work out in advance where the various colours will appear. A maximum of four colours should be used in any one design; any more may prove difficult to handle. Trace the outline on to thin paper. Cut similar-sized pieces of fabric and stack them so that the least-used colours are at the bottom. Place the pattern on top and tack (baste) through all the layers; be sure that they all lie flat.

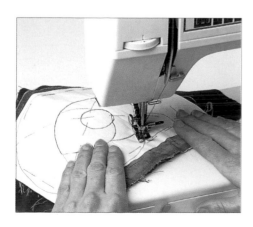

2 Set the sewing machine to a medium-length straight stitch and sew accurately over the pattern outline. Gently tear away the tissue paper, without pulling the thread.

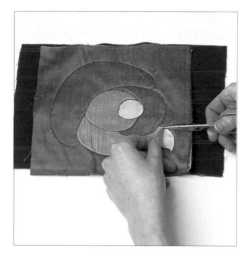

3 Using a pair of sharp, pointed embroidery scissors, begin to cut away the fabric. Cut just inside the stitch line, leaving a very narrow margin, and be careful not to snip the stitches.

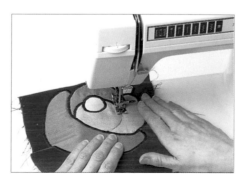

4 Sew over the outline a second time, using a broad satin stitch in a contrasting thread. The stitch can be tapered at points or sharp angles by adjusting the width. Be sure that the stitching covers the raw edges on both sides of the line, trimming them back further if necessary. Neaten the finished piece by pulling the ends of thread through to the back and tying them.

73

Felt Appliqué

Felt is a long-established favourite for appliqué; it is easy to handle and, because it is not woven, it does not fray. Detailed motifs can be cut freehand or from templates, then tacked (basted) down and attached to the background with a machine zigzag or a hand embroidery stitch. Using iron-on fusible bonding saves time and gives a professional effect; the pattern is drawn directly on to the paper backing, so the shapes are always accurate.

Above: Many kinds of decoration or detail can be added to felt appliqué. This confetti-like garland was inspired by the shapes of Japanese cookie cutters. The individual flowers are sewn with contrasting threads, and finished with tiny pearl beads.

1 Trace the separate elements of the design on to the bonding, allowing for any overlap. Remember that the finished pattern will have to be reversed if it is not symmetrical.

2 Roughly cut out each shape and place them, paper side up, on felt of the appropriate colour. Cover with a damp cloth and iron on using a pressing action.

3 When the felt has cooled and the adhesive set, cut out accurately around the outline.

Above: In the nineteenth century, felt was used to make ornamental table covers to protect polished wooden furniture from everyday wear. These often combined patchwork and appliqué, and were embellished with embroidery. Flowers and hearts were especially popular and this motif is adapted from a cloth made in the north of England. The raised petals and the leaves are edged with blanket stitch worked in a single strand of crewel yarn.

4 Peel off the backing paper. Fix down the background shapes first, again using a pressing cloth and a medium heat setting. Build up the rest of the design, one piece at a time.

Reverse Felt Appliqué

The non-fraying qualities of felt make it ideal for reverse appliqué because there is no need to turn under or conceal the raw edges of the fabric. More layers can be used and more colours introduced: the technique example uses four pieces of felt. Small, sharp embroidery scissors are essential for cutting through the felt – the curved blades of nail scissors are suitable for the finest detail.

Right: This three-dimensional nursery rhyme illustration is deceptively naive in appearance; the method used to produce it is innovative and skilful. Seven different colours of felt have been used and, as the layers have been cut into, a great feeling of depth has been produced.

1 Pin and tack (baste) the felt together, with white on the bottom, then blue, pink and a slightly larger square of black. Transfer the design on to the white layer. With black thread sew along the guides and around the outer edge of the square in straight stitch. This stitching needs to be strong, so it worth going over the outline twice. Fasten the ends securely on the white side.

2 Turn the work over so the black side is facing. Cut away the first layer, as close to the stitched lines as possible, so that the felt that is left forms a thin neat line, defining the design.

3 Remove more of the felt from other parts of the design, cutting through either one or two layers to reveal the colours below.

4 Stitch in the fine detail by hand. Cut-out flowers can be added to the background. Sew down in the centre only, using French knots in contrasting thread, to give a raised effect.

Pattern Cut Appliqué

The simple fold and cut techniques that are used by children to make snowflakes and paper chains have been adapted by quilt-makers all over the world. The resulting designs are striking and symmetrical, and relatively quick to sew. The best known of these whole-cloth appliqués are Hawaiian quilts which are cut from a single sheet of fabric. This technique can be simplified to produce bold and interesting patterns. Solid colours on a white background are most effective. Spend time experimenting with different designs, remembering not to cut through the folds and to leave a narrow turning around the edges. Soft curves and flowing lines are easiest to work with and fine-weave cottons the best choice of fabric.

Above: Two vibrantly opposed colours are used for this Egyptian appliqué, which draws its imagery from Islamic art. The design has been cut from several pieces of blue cotton, appliquéd onto a contrasting pink background cloth.

1 This eight-pointed daisy medallion is taken from a turkey red and white coverlet, made in Ireland during the 1870s. Start by folding the top fabric in half, then into quarters, then eighths.

2 Pin a pattern template to the folded fabric and cut out.

3 Turn under a seam allowance of 6mm (¼in) all round and tack (baste) down.

4 Pin, then tack (baste) to the background fabric, ensuring that the motif lies flat. Sew down with small slip stitches in a matching thread.

Left: This Indian cushion cover is made from two pieces of cloth: a dark background fabric and a fine white cotton which has been folded into squares and cut to produce a geometric repeat pattern. Large canopies and bedspreads are made in this way.

San Blas Appliqué

The most complex form of reverse appliqué is South American seminole work, a multicoloured technique developed by the women of the San Blas Islands, off the Panamanian coast. It was originally worked in small panels known as *mola* cloth and used to decorate garments, but is now made for export as a more commercial concern. The imagery used is pictorial, derived from mythology, folklore and the makers' natural surroundings. Up to ten different colours can appear in a single piece; a simplified way of working is illustrated.

Above: The gently curving lines of this stylized fish are suited to reverse appliqué. These are echoed by the shape of the formalized blue waves, which are made from lightly padded bias strips. The slit and circle background patterns are typical of San Blas work.

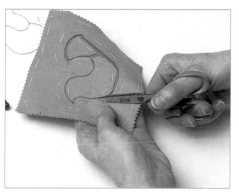

1 Tack (baste) the first two layers together and transfer the design to the top. Thin fabrics which do not fray easily, such as cotton lawn, should be used and they should all be of a similar weight. The darkest colours are placed towards the top, to prevent the turned-under edges from showing through. Tack (baste) around either side of the outline, then cut along it with sharp-pointed embroidery scissors.

2 Using the point of the needle to turn under a narrow hem, slip stitch the edges of the top fabric to the layer below.

3 Tack (baste) the third colour to the top of the work and, feeling through the cloth, trace over the hemmed edge of the main shape. Cut out around this outline to expose the two layers below. Turn under the raw edges as before.

4 Ordinary hand appliqué can be used to add detail.

Left: This intricate appliqué was made by the Yao people, a hill tribe of northern Thailand. It uses a cut-away technique, very similar to San Blas work, but the colours are subtler and the pattern more complicated, reflecting differences between the two cultures. Satin stitch is used to emphasize the design and the centre panel is embroidered in cross stitch.

Knitting

Like all other needlecrafts, knitting has been practised for many centuries, in many parts of the world, although its exact origins are obscure. Textiles have always been made to be used and worn, so little remains from the ancient and more recent past. Fragments of knitted-type fabrics have been discovered in pre-dynastic tombs in Egypt, but it is believed that these were formed by needle-weaving with separate strands of yarn, rather than knitted from a single length. It is known, however, that the nomads of the Middle East spun wool from their sheep and knitted it into intricately patterned garments and tent flaps. These travelling people took their craft from place to place and traders introduced it to Mediterranean seaports, from where it spread to western Europe.

During early times knitting was worked on simple peg-board frames, in the same way that children's French knitting cords are made today. The changeover to using four needles for working in the round came about some two thousand years ago. It was only in later years that metal needles were manufactured; they were first made of sharpened wood, and there

are even records of goose quills being adapted for knitting.

In Europe, by the Middle Ages, knitting had become an almost exclusively male preserve, and women were employed in spinning the yarn. Knitting guilds were established in most capital cities to protect craft skills – and their members were all men. The entry standards were as rigorous as for any other craft; an apprentice had to study for six years to be judged proficient enough to join a guild, and he had to create several items for assessment, including silk stockings, a multicoloured carpet and a felted cap. At this time knitting was closely linked with felt-making. Circular hats were made from thick woollen yarn, which was then washed, pounded and moulded to create a warm and densely textured fabric.

The knitting industry became mechanized well before the Industrial

Revolution, although hand knitting continued in outlying areas where sheep were bred. In the 1600s, the Reverend William Lee invented a machine for manufacturing stockings, which used a ring of latchet hooks. All knitting machines still use the same principle. The first hose he produced were of thick wool, but he refined the machinery so that delicate silk could be made into stockings that met with the approval of Queen Elizabeth I.

As knitting became widespread, distinctive regional and national variations emerged. Cardigans from the Austrian Tyrol were embroidered with spring flowers, while the heavy-duty sweaters needed to keep out the freezing Norwegian winter winds were decorated with reindeer and fir trees. Scandinavian patterns are predominantly white, like the snow, with dark primary coloured motifs, but traditional Spanish knitting, with

Modern knitting can be very adventurous: these brightly striped hats for adults and children are bold and sculptural in form.

The softly muted autumnal shades of this traditional Shetland hat and glove set come from using natural undyed fleece to spin the wool.

Left: The vivid colours of a medieval stained glass window were the inspiration behind this beautifully hand-knitted intarsia design.

Wales, but their origins date back many centuries. Local legend has it that the multicoloured banded designs were inspired by the knitted garments worn by sailors of the Spanish Armada, whose ships had been wrecked on the treacherous Shetland

its North African influence, used the brightest silk yarns with extra gold and silver threads.

The characteristic knitted garments still produced on the Shetland Isles are well known for the expertise that goes into making them. The classic geometric pullovers were highly sought after in the 1930s, when they became the trademark of the then Prince of

coast. Shetland knitting has now developed into a thriving local industry and the fleece is processed and spun on the islands. Most of the knitters work from their own homes to produce garments and heirloom lace shawls, which are exported worldwide. It is only recently that many of the patterns have been written down and charted; previously knitters had learnt them by memory in childhood.

Sailors and fishermen everywhere have always needed to wear practical and waterproof sweaters. The textured motifs usually include anchors, along with twisted cables that represent the ropes and nets which they used every day. The potential of these exclusively male garments was recognized in the 1900s when long, elegant variations of the traditional Jerseys and Guernseys from the Channel Islands were adopted by emancipated women. The ancient cable, bobble and diamond patterns of the Aran islanders, traditionally knitted in unbleached cream wool, have been revived several times since the 1950s, and are as popular now as they have ever been.

The long-established textured Aran patterns of interlaced cables and bobbles have been reinterpreted in soft yarns to make these contemporary sweaters.

Knitting
Tools and Materials

To the beginner, the tremendous array of yarns available may seem quite bewildering. Wools should be chosen with the end purpose in mind but all printed patterns give a recommended yarn, needle-size and tension (gauge).

KNITTING NEEDLES

There are three types of needle: single-pointed, double-pointed and circular. Single-pointed needles are used for most work and range from 2.00 to 10.00mm in diameter; the finest are made from metal and the thicker ones from plastic. Bamboo needles are more flexible and therefore easier on the hands. Large garment pieces and tubular knitting are worked on circular needles. Sets of four double-pointed needles are also used for small circular pieces such as socks or hats. Cable needles carry groups of stitches across the surface of the knitting.

TOOLS AND ACCESSORIES

Stitch counters record the number of rows worked and stitch markers can be slipped over the needles to indicate where a row begins in circular knitting. Use a gauge to check needle sizes – this is particularly useful as old needles were numbered to a different system. A crochet hook is useful for picking up dropped stitches and tapestry needles are used to stitch pieces together and for tidying up ends.

YARN

Knitting yarns come in many colours and textures, and are made from natural, synthetic and blended fibres. Wool and acrylic are warm and practical, and combinations of the two are specially formulated for easy washing. Constantly developing processes mean that new "novelty" yarns are always on the market.

Yarns are classified according to weight – light, medium or heavy – and by the number of threads or plys which are spun together to make the strand. Basic double knitting is a versatile 4-ply wool and 3-ply "fingering" is used for baby garments. Fine Shetland lace is knitted from 2-ply wool which comes in subtle natural colours. Cotton yarns are also made in several weights.

Thick bouclé.

Shetland single-ply.

Chenille.

Cotton yarn.

Space-dyed yarn.

Double knitting.

Chunky synthetics.

Textured and novelty yarns.

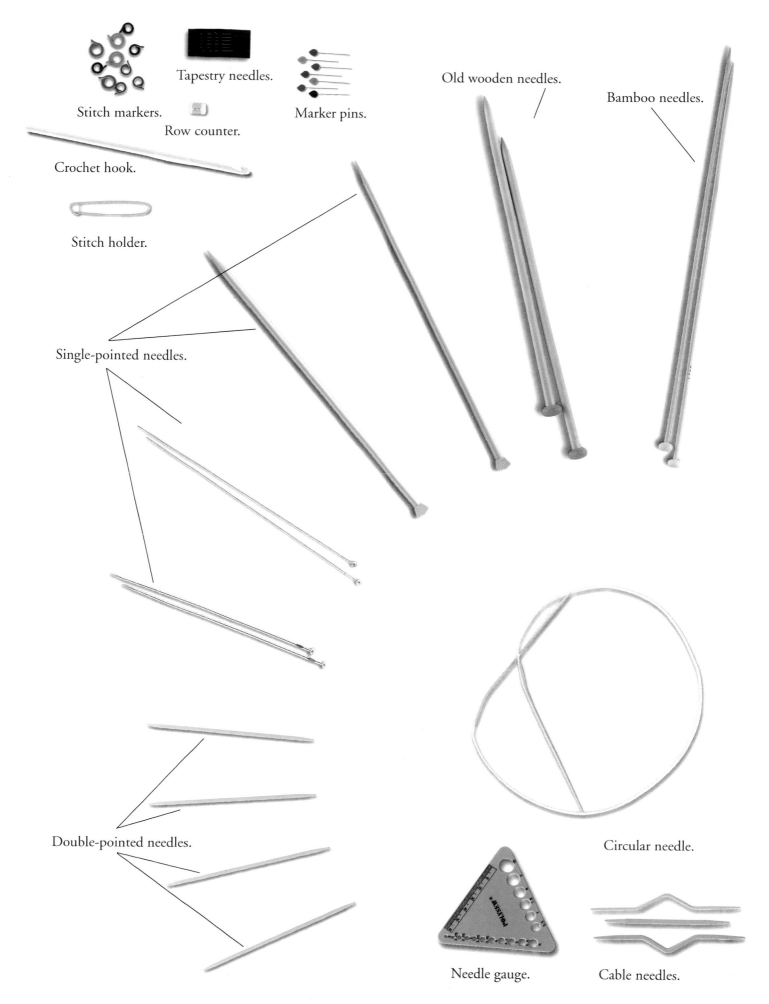

Stitch markers.

Tapestry needles.

Marker pins.

Row counter.

Crochet hook.

Stitch holder.

Single-pointed needles.

Double-pointed needles.

Old wooden needles.

Bamboo needles.

Circular needle.

Needle gauge.

Cable needles.

81

Casting On

Knitting is worked on two needles and the fabric grows as the stitches are passed from one to the other. There are no set rules about how to hold the yarn and needles – knitters in different parts of the world use them in entirely different ways – and, with practice, everybody finds their own personal method. Left-handed workers should use a mirror to reverse the technique pictures.

Plain stocking stitch is all that has been used here to create these exciting swatches, which are knitted from a selection of fashion yarns.

CASTING ON

The knitted stitches are built up on a foundation of loops. The two most common ways of making this initial row are the one-needle and the two-needle method. The first, sometimes called the thumb method, is perhaps the easiest for beginners and gives an elastic, hardwearing edge. Whichever technique is chosen, it is important to work with an even tension, or the stitches will be too tight to work.

Both methods of casting on begin with a slip loop, which forms the first stitch.

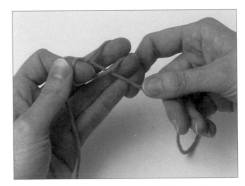

1 MAKING A SLIP LOOP Wrap the long end of the yarn around the short end.

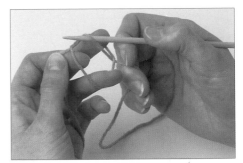

2 Use the tip of the needle to lift the main strand through the loop.

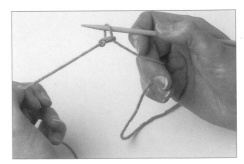

3 Pull on the short end to tighten the slip loop.

1 ONE-NEEDLE METHOD
Make a slip loop at the end of the yarn, allowing at least 30cm (6in) plus an extra 2.5cm (1in) for each stitch. Place the loop on the needle and hold in the right hand. Wrap the short end under and over the left fingers and hold securely in place with the thumb.

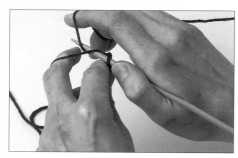

2 Insert the tip of the needle under the yarn between the first and second fingers, then with the right hand, wrap the long end of the yarn under and over the needle.

3 Bring the needle and yarn forward, under the taut thread, pulling with the left hand to tighten the new stitch that has been made.

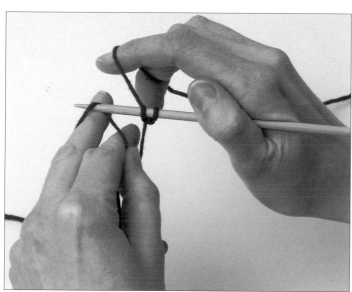

4 Repeat the process for the next stitch and continue until the required number of stitches has been made.

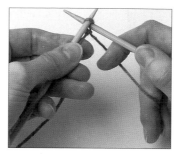

1 TWO-NEEDLE METHOD
Make a slip loop 30cm (6in) from the end of the yarn and place on the left needle. Insert the right needle through the loop from front to back. Hold the working yarn in the right hand, keeping the tension by passing it under the middle two fingers and around the little finger.

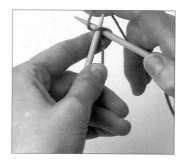

2 With the right hand, wrap the yarn forward, under and over the right needle.

3 This forms the new loop: draw it through the slip loop with the tip of the right needle.

4 Pass the new loop on to the left-hand needle, next to the slip loop.

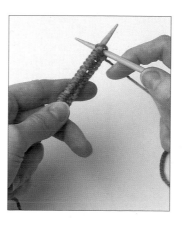

5 Insert the right needle through the front of the new stitch, wrap the yarn under and over the tip, then repeat the process to make another stitch. Continue until the required number of stitches has been made.

Knit and Purl

There are just two stitches – knit and purl – which form the basis of all knitting patterns. When a stitch is knitted, the loop lies at the back of the finished work so that the front of the stitch has a flat appearance; when a stitch is purled the loop lies to the front of the work, so that a small raised line is formed.

Above: Garter stitch is the simplest of all stitches and is formed when every stitch of each row is knitted. The work is reversible and has an elastic texture, ideal for blankets, scarves or sweaters.

1 KNIT STITCH The working needle is held in the right hand, in the same way as a pencil. Maintain tension by passing the yarn over the first finger, under the two middle fingers and loosely around the little finger. It should pass through easily. Insert the right needle through the first loop on the left needle, from front to back.

Above: Striped patterns can easily be created by changing the yarn colour between rows.

2 The point of the right needle is now lying behind the left needle. Wrap the yarn forward, under and over the right needle.

3 Bring the point of the right needle forward, down and under the left needle, drawing the yarn through to make a new stitch.

4 Slip the new stitch off the left needle and on to the right. Repeat until all the stitches have been knitted. Continue with the next row by turning the work and swapping the needles over.

STOCKING (STOCKINETTE) STITCH is most commonly used for garments and has a horizontal stretch. It is formed by knitting one row and purling the next, which produces its distinctively smooth "right" side.

REVERSE STOCKING (STOCKINETTE) STITCH is really the "wrong" side of stocking (stockinette) stitch, and has the appearance of a dense garter stitch. It is used as a contrast pattern, particularly in fisherman's sweater patterns.

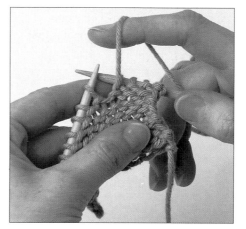

1 PURL STITCH
Bring the yarn to the front of the work and across the right needle.

2 Insert the tip of the right needle from right to left through the next stitch on the left needle.

3 Wrap the yarn back over the right needle, from right to left between the two points, and back under the right needle to the front.

4 Slide the point of the right needle down and back behind the tip of the left needle and slip the new stitch on to the right needle. Continue to the end of the row.

Following a Pattern

At first glance, any knitting pattern may appear to be just a string of complicated codes, but it is actually set out in a logical and concise form. A standard series of abbreviations and symbols is used to guide the worker through each row of the pattern: those used in this book are given here, although all printed patterns will include their own key.

Read the pattern carefully and be sure of the instructions before embarking on any new project. For the best results use the yarn specified, where possible. Different dye lots may vary in colour so read the label on each ball to make sure they match.

ABBREVIATIONS

beg	beginning
c	cable
cont	continue
dec	decrease
foll	following
inc	increase
K	knit
K2tog	knit 2 together
K2tog tbl	knit 2 together through back of loop
m1	make 1
patt (pat)	pattern
P	purl
P2tog	purl 2 together
psso	pass slip stitch over
RS	right side
rep	repeat
sl st	slip stitch
sts	stitches
tog	together
WS	wrong side
yrn (yo)	yarn round needle (yarn over needle)
yfwd (yf)	yarn forward
( )	repeat the instructions inside the brackets for the number of times indicated
*	repeat the instructions that follow the asterisk

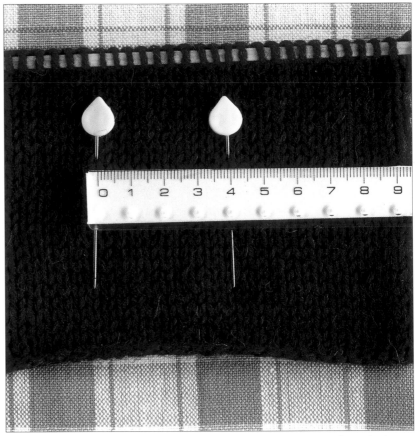

Marker pins and a ruler are used to measure the number of stitches.

TENSION (GAUGE)

It is important to knit with the proper tension or gauge. This does not only mean working evenly, so that all the stitches are regular, but also ensuring that the work meets the measurements given in the pattern. Tension (gauge) determines the size of the stitch, and therefore the finished size of the knitted garment, so it is vital that it is correct.

Tension (gauge) is measured by knitting up a sample using the needle size and yarn specified by the designer and this should always be done before starting to make up any new project. Most patterns name a particular brand of yarn and the design will be sized with this in mind. If another yarn is substituted, it is even more necessary to check tension (gauge) first. The pattern will specify the amount of stitches which, when worked over a set number of rows, should reach a given measurement.

Work up the swatch, which should be at least 10cm (4in) square and pin it out on a flat surface without stretching it in any direction. Measure and mark out the given width and carefully count the number of whole stitches that lie within it. Count the number of rows in the same way. If there are not enough stitches, the tension (gauge) is too tight and needles one size larger should be used; if there are too many, the work is too loose and needles a size smaller should be used. Continue experimenting with different needles until the sample meets the correct tension (gauge). If it does not, the finished garment will be the wrong size and a lot of time and effort will have been wasted.

Knitting Gallery

There are many options open to the imaginative knitter. The selection of patterns available caters for every taste and level of skill. Specialist designers produce kits to make high-fashion garments, but even the plainest knitted sweater can be embellished with embroidery beads. The examples illustrated here should inspire some original ideas.

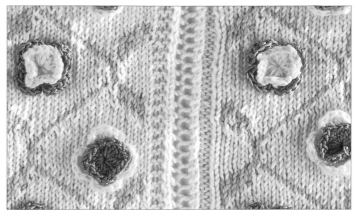

To create this delicate trellis pattern, pink and yellow crochet flower motifs have been appliquéd on to a hand-knitted background.

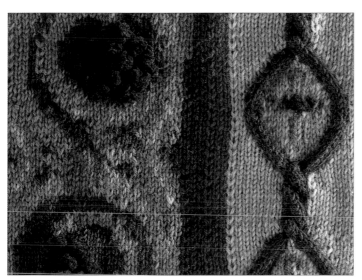

The raised texture of these bobble stitch grapes is emphasized by the choice of a velvety chenille yarn in a rich purple.

Traditional Fair Isle knitting draws on the imagery of nature; the geometric shapes on these gloves are reminiscent of snowflakes.

Woven carpets and other textiles from many cultures can be a great source of inspiration for intarsia knitting and the designs can be charted on to squared paper.

Small silver beads and subtle gold yarn provide delicate highlights on this floral pattern, which has a medieval simplicity.

Natural wooden beads have been applied to a textured background knitted from unbleached cotton in a mixture of stitches.

Correcting Mistakes

As with any new skill, all beginners are bound to make mistakes when starting to knit. It takes time to learn how to control the yarn and needles with confidence, and it may help to ask an experienced knitter for guidance. Dropped stitches, however, are easily corrected, or picked up, with the needles. They may slip off if the work is set aside in the middle of a row or if it has been knitted hastily. Sometimes a dropped stitch may go unnoticed and form a ladder, which will have to be picked up with a crochet hook.

1 PICKING UP A PURL STITCH The dropped stitch is corrected by passing the loose yarn back through it.

1 PICKING UP A KNIT STITCH The dropped stitch will need to be brought back up to the same level as the rest of the row.

2 Insert the right needle through the front of the loose stitch, from front to back and under the strand of the yarn.

2 Insert the right needle through the front of the loose stitch from front to back, without twisting it, and under the strand of yarn behind it.

3 Insert the left needle through the stitch from front to back and lift it over the strand, keeping the stitch on the right needle.

3 Use the tip of the left needle to lift the stitch over the yarn, keeping the new loop on the right needle.

4 Slip the new stitch back on to the left needle, ready to continue with a purl row.

PICKING UP A LADDER
Knit stitch Insert a crochet hook through the front of the first dropped stitch and pull the loose strand from behind through the loop to form a new stitch. Repeat to the top of the ladder and slip the last stitch on to the left needle.

4 Place the tip of the left needle through the front of the stitch from left to right and slide it back on to the needle, ready to be re-knitted.

Purl stitch The method is the same as for knit stitch, but the hook is inserted from behind the work.

Casting Off

A piece of knitting is completed by casting off the stitches. This is usually done on the right side of the work and knit stitches should be cast off knitwise and purl stitches purlwise. This is especially important when casting off the ribbing at a cuff or neck edge. If the cast-off stitches are too tight they will distort the work, but using a larger size needle can help to make a looser finish. There are several specialized ways of casting off, but the method shown here is the most common and straightforward.

Above: The cast-off edge gives a neat selvage to the knitted piece. The loose yarn from the beginning and end should be sewn invisibly along the edge of the work.

1 CASTING OFF KNITWISE Knit the first two stitches as usual.

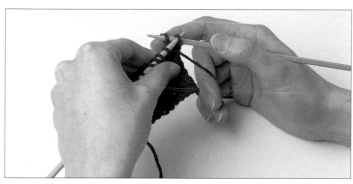

2 Insert the left needle under the first stitch made, from left to right.

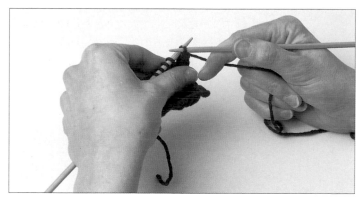

3 Lift the stitch up and over the second stitch and over the point of the right needle. The first stitch has now been cast off.

4 Knit the next stitch from the left needle so that there are two stitches on the right needle. Lift the first stitch over the second and continue casting off to the end of the row. Cut the end of the yarn and draw it through the final stitch to finish off.

CASTING OFF PURLWISE The method is the same for casting off a purl row: purl two stitches and lift the first stitch over the second as before.

Knitted Pattern Stitches

Knitting has a rich heritage of pattern stitches which incorporates intricate cables, eyelets or raised bobbles, and knitwear designers are constantly developing new ideas. There are, however, many interesting textured patterns that can be created simply by combining knit and purl stitches to produce a textured surface. Moss stitch variations give a firm, reversible fabric while rib stitch gives a stretchy vertical stripe, used to finish the welts (bottom), cuffs and neck edges of sweaters. To ensure a snug fit, it is usually worked with needles a size smaller than those used for the main part of the garment. Horizontal furrows are formed by working alternate stripes of stocking and garter stitch.

Embossed textures show to best advantage when plain yarns, such as natural cottons, are used.

THREE BY THREE RIB This is worked over a multiple of six stitches, plus three.

Row 1 *K3, P3; rep from *, K3
Row 2 P3, *K3, P3p; rep from *
These two rows form the pattern.

RIDGED BANDS These are worked over any number of stitches.

Row 1 Knit
Row 2 Purl
Rows 3 and 4 Knit
Row 5 Purl
Row 6 Knit
Repeat these six rows to form the pattern.

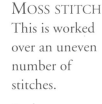

MOSS STITCH This is worked over an uneven number of stitches.

Each row as follows: *K1, P1; rep from *, K1.

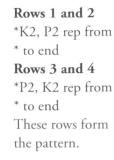

DOUBLE MOSS STITCH This is worked over a multiple of four stitches.

Rows 1 and 2 *K2, P2 rep from * to end
Rows 3 and 4 *P2, K2 rep from * to end
These rows form the pattern.

FISHERMAN'S SWEATER PATTERNS

Knit and purl patterns were traditionally used by the women of seafaring villages to ornament the sweaters worn by local fishermen. These garments were the main protection from the elements in the days before weatherproof clothing and had to stand up to hard physical wear. The various ports and fishing villages around the coasts of many countries evolved their own individual variations of diamond, zigzag or chevron panels, which are still design classics today.

BASKET WEAVE
This is worked over a multiple of eight stitches, plus five.

Row 1 (RS) knit
Row 2 K5, *P3, K5; rep from *
Row 3 P5, *K3, P5; rep from *
Row 4 as row 2
Row 5 Knit
Row 6 K1, *P3, K5; rep from *, to last 4 sts, P3, K1
Row 7 P1, *K3, P5; rep from *, to last 4 sts, K3, P1
Row 8 as row 6
These eight rows form the pattern.

EMBOSSED LADDER PATTERN
This is worked over a multiple of 14 stitches.

Row 1 *K1, P2, K1, P1, K2, P2, K2, P2, K1, rep from *
Row 2 *(P1, K2) twice, P2, (K2, P1) twice, rep from *
Row 3 *K1, P2, K2, P2, K2, P1, K1, P2, K1, rep from *
Row 4 *P1, K2, P3, K2, P3, K2, P1, rep from *
These four rows form the pattern.

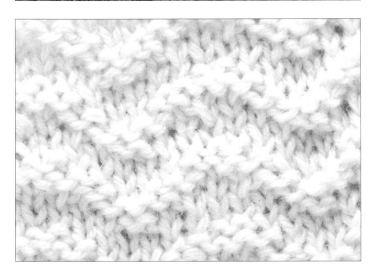

WAVE STITCH
This is worked over a multiple of eight stitches, plus six.

Row 1 (RS) K6, *P2, K6; rep from *
Row 2 K1, *P4, K4, rep from *, end P4, K1
Row 3 P2, *K2, P2; rep from *
Row 4 P1, *K4, P4; rep from *, end K4, P1
Row 5 K2, *P2, K6; rep from *, end P2, K2
Row 6 P6, *K2, P6; rep from *
Row 7 P1, *K4, P4, rep from *, end K4, P1
Row 8 K2, *P2, K2; rep from *
Row 9 K1, *P4, K4; rep from *, end P4, K1
Row 10 P2, *K2, P6, rep from *, end K2, P2
These ten rows form the pattern.

ZIGZAG
This is worked over a multiple of six stitches.

Row 1 (WS) and all other odd rows, Purl
Row 2 *K3, P3, rep from *
Row 4 P1, *K3, P3, rep from *, end K3, P2
Row 6 P2, *K3, P3; rep from *, end K3, P1
Row 8 *P3, K3; rep from *
Row 10 P2, *K3, P3; rep from *, end K3, P1
Row 12 P1, *K3, P3; rep from *, end K3, P2
These 12 rows form the pattern.

Increasing and Decreasing

A piece of knitting is shaped as it is worked, by alternating the number of stitches on the needles. In effect, the width is increased by adding more stitches to the row and decreased by taking some away. There are several ways in which this can be done, depending on the type of fabric being knitted. The effect can be almost invisible, or give a decorative openwork effect.

1 DECREASING *Knit two together (K2tog)* The simplest way of decreasing is to work two stitches together, at either end, or in the middle of a row. The method for purling two stitches together is similar. At the start of the row, insert the needle from right to left through the first two stitches. Knit as usual. This gives a slant to the right.

2 Knit two together at the end of a row by inserting the needle from left to right through the last two stitches. This produces a slant to the left. It creates an invisible shaping and is used for sleeves as a paired decrease, one side sloping to the right and one to the left.

Above: When lacy fabric, such as these delicate single-ply Shetland scarves, is being knitted, the number of stitches must remain constant, so for every one that is decreased, another is created.

1 *Slipped stitch method (Sl1, K1, Psso)* At the beginning of a row, slip the first stitch on to the right needle without knitting it.

2 Knit the next stitch as usual.

3 Insert the left needle through the slipped stitch and lift it up, across the knitted stitch and off the end of the needle.

4 At the end of a row, slip the last but one stitch, knit the final stitch and pass the slip stitch over the knitted stitch.

INCREASING

Increasing between stitches (M1k) The extra stitch for this invisible method comes from working into the horizontal strand of yarn that lies between two stitches.

Bar Method An additional stitch can also be made by knitting twice into the same loop. This does not give as smooth an appearance as the previous method, so it is used at seam edges.

1 With the right needle, lift the horizontal strand between the last knitted stitch and the next and place it on to the left needle.

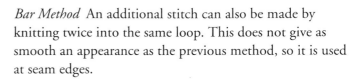

1 Knit the stitch as usual, but keep it on the left needle.

2 Knit into the back of the strand, to twist and tighten the loop.

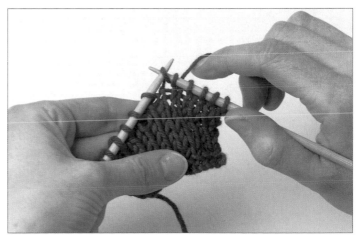

2 Insert the right needle into the back of the stitch just knitted and knit it again.

3 Slip the new stitch on to the right needle.

3 Slip the double stitch on to the right needle.

Working with Colour

A limitless range of multicoloured patterns, from traditional Fair Isle, to contemporary intarsia or Jacquard designs, can be created by combining different yarns. Stripes are the quickest and easiest way to introduce colour and can be boldly contrasting or subtly shaded. The Fair Isle way of working appears to be very complex, but, in fact, the intricate patterns are cleverly designed so that only two yarns are required in any one row.

JOINING COLOUR AT THE START OF A ROW

This is a quick method of working with two colours of yarn to create a horizontally striped fabric. Any loose ends can be sewn in when the piece is finished.

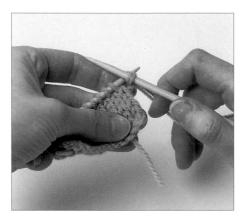

1 Insert the right needle as usual at the beginning of the yarn. Leaving an end of roughly 30cm (6in), loop the new colour over the needle with the old. Knit the stitch.

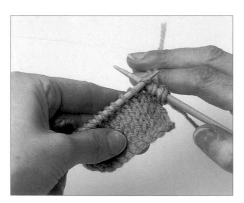

2 Let the first yarn drop to the side, knit the next two stitches with the double new yarn, then knit the rest of the row with the single strand of new yarn.

3 Carry the loose ends of the yarn along the outside edge as the stripes are knitted.

Above: Multicoloured designs are usually worked from a chart on which one square corresponds to one stitch. These are straightforward to draw up, when designing original patterns, and can be filled in with coloured pencils. Many printed patterns are in black and white, and a series of symbols are used to represent the various colours.

JOINING COLOUR WITHIN A ROW

Intarsia patterns may require yarn to be joined within a row to create new areas of colour. Sew in the short ends later.

1 Leaving the first yarn at the back of the work, loop the new colour over the needle and knit the next stitch.

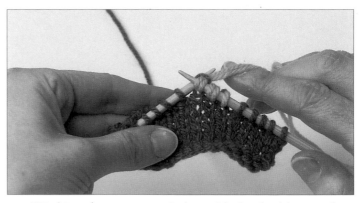

2 Working the next two stitches with the double yarn, let the short end drop and continue with the single yarn.

INTARSIA

When two blocks of colour meet within a row, the two yarns must be twisted together to give a smooth finish and to prevent holes appearing.

CARRYING YARN ACROSS THE BACK

When two colours appear in the same row, only one is actually in use at any one time, so the second colour has to be carried across the back. This creates loose strands, or floats, which can pull and distort, so to maintain an even tension (gauge) they must be woven into the work every few stitches.

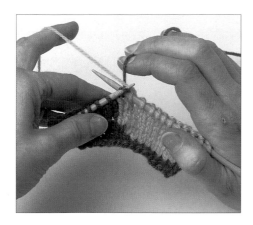

1 On knit rows, hold the first colour across the back of the work to the left and work the next stitch with the second colour so that the yarn passes over the taut strand.

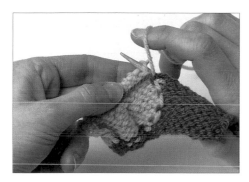

2 On purl rows, hold the first colour across to the left and pass the second colour over it before purling the next stitch.

1 On a knit row, hold the floating colour out to the left so that the working yarn passes over it before knitting the next stitch.

2 On a purl row, hold the floating yarn up between the points of the two needles so that the working yarn goes across it before purling the next stitch.

3 Be sure that the float then drops clear of the working yarn, while it is being used.

The different yarns in the traditional Fair Isle Symbister pattern are varied from dark to light by "shading in" the colour in interlocking rows of small diamonds.

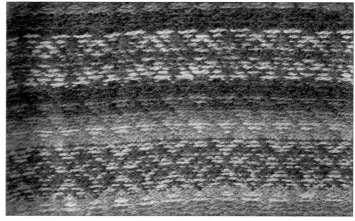

The back of the sweater shows how the colours are carried across, so that no loop extends for more than three stitches.

Crochet

Crochet is an adaptable and enjoyable craft. It can be worked in many different yarns and on various scales to produce a surprising range of items, both simple and elaborate. Its name originates from the French *croche*, or hook, and a crochet hook and a ball of yarn are all that is needed. Crochet is made throughout the world: women of the Mediterranean specialize in fine lace; in parts of Africa it is used to make special caps that denote status, and in China fine crochet table linen is made for export.

The exact origins of crochet are uncertain, but it is known that "the art of the crochet needle" was widespread throughout seventeenth-century Europe. At that time most fine needlework was produced within convents, particularly in Italy. Lace, embroidery and crochet were known as Nuns' Work and highly prized by the outside world. The patterns were based on needlepoint and bobbin lace designs and crocheted in the finest linen thread. The sisters taught their skills to members of the neighbouring communities and crochet spread to Ireland via the church, where it was used to adorn religious vestments and altar cloths.

This Scandinavian-style heart border makes an attractive shelf-edging that would look at home in the bedroom or kitchen.

A flourishing cottage industry existed around the counties of Cork and Carrickmacross, producing Irish Point, Raised Rose and Honiton Crochet. These delicate laces were based on natural motifs: roses, leaves and trefoils. As early as 1743 the Royal Dublin Society awarded prizes for crochet, which was done by both men and women. When the potato famine of 1847 brought economic depression to the country, crochet proved the sole source of income for many people. Some workers were able to earn enough from the craft to pay their passage to a new life in America. Those who remained in Ireland were encouraged to make exquisite lace, which was sold to the landed gentry and taken to London couture houses. Irish crochet was a very popular

fashion item and high prices were paid for extravagant collars and cuffs.

Mercerization processes were developed which gave stronger and more lustrous threads, and more designs appeared. *Beeton's Book of Needlework*, the most celebrated and widely sold manual of its time, was lavish in its praise: "Crochet is easy to work and its strength, durability, and the numerous uses to which it may be applied ensure its lasting hold on the feminine mind."

By the turn of the century crochet was arguably the most popular domestic craft. Lengths of white lace were used to trim petticoats, bloomers and camisoles, as well as outer garments, while crochet lace gloves, bags and parasols were essential accessories. Crochet was not only used

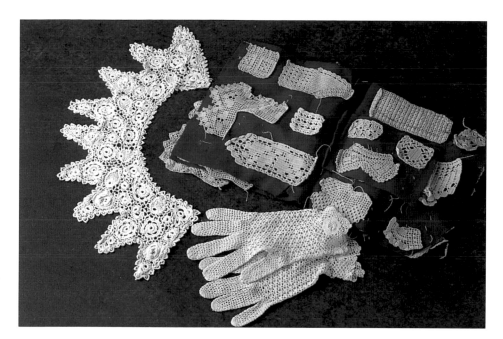

Left: This antique Irish crochet collar and gloves are typical of the fine work that was produced in the nineteenth century. The red flannel sample book was used as a pattern reference source.

the craft was not really revived until the 1960s, when it took on a whole new character. Bright psychedelic colours were used to make mini-skirts, tabards and tank tops. Geometric Op Art motifs were adapted for crochet bedspreads, cushions and rugs.

This style may seem unfashionable now, as the crazes of previous generations always do, but crochet is a flexible medium. Designers are now

Right: Household string is just one of the unexpected yarns that can be crocheted. Simple rows of half-trebles make this functional pencil case.

Above: In this traditional traycloth design, circular flower-shaped motifs are joined together with tiny squares.

for decorating clothing, but was also used in the home to edge blinds, bed linen and dressing-table sets, tablecloths and napkins, chairbacks and doileys. Cotton crochet was hardwearing and withstood repeated laundering and ironing. Many instruction and pattern books were published and crochet was practised by women across all social groups.

Elaborate Victorian designs had been replaced by a more sophisticated style, for both dress and furnishings. Magazine editors dictated plain edges on tablecloths, rather than ornamental scalloped or zigzag borders, while the influence of Art Nouveau was seen in a more naturalistic representation of flowers. Small pictorial motifs were made as insets for traycloths or nightdress cases and narrow ribbon insertions were popular.

Interest in crochet had waned by the 1930s. Functional woollen garments and blankets, cotton dishcloths and pot holders continued to be made, but

looking back for ideas, which can be adapted in a new way, with new yarns, and many exciting and desirable patterns are currently available.

These endearing three-dimensional insects, made from coloured raffia, are an example of the innovative crochet that is being produced by contemporary designers.

97

Crochet
Tools and Materials

String.

Metallic yarns.

Raffia.

Fine cottons.

A simple ball of yarn and a hook are all that is needed to begin to crochet. Any wool or cotton yarns can be used, as well as more unusual materials such as string or raffia, but in addition, there is a selection of special crochet cottons for creating more delicate fabrics.

YARNS

Crochet cottons come in balls and are sold by weight. They are numbered from No 3, which is the thickest 2-ply thread, known as craft cotton, up to No 60, which is a firmly twisted 6-ply, used for the finest lace. Space-dyed variations are available for interesting multicoloured effects. No 20 is a thicker 6-ply yarn used for most mats, edgings and traditional white work, but it is also available in other colours. Perlé thread, similar to embroidery thread, has a lustrous mercerized finish. Cotton double knitting yarns form hard wearing fabrics, suitable for bags and placemats or larger projects such as bedspreads. Novelty yarns work up into light and airy garments while metallic yarns come in different weights and colours, perfect for evening wear.

HOOKS

The finer the yarn used, the smaller the hook needed. Like knitting needles, crochet hooks are graded from a delicate 0.75mm up to 10.00mm, which is used for working strip rugs or for creating open, "loopy" textiles. The smallest are made from steel, the larger sizes from resilient plastic. Some workers find that wooden-handled or all-wood hooks are easier to hold. The best hooks have smooth edges that do not snag the wool. In the past, hooks were turned from bone and examples of these can still be found in antique shops. Basic sewing tools are also necessary: a selection of needles is useful for sewing in ends and for joining seams, and small sharp scissors will be needed to cut threads.

Textured yarns.

Crochet cottons.

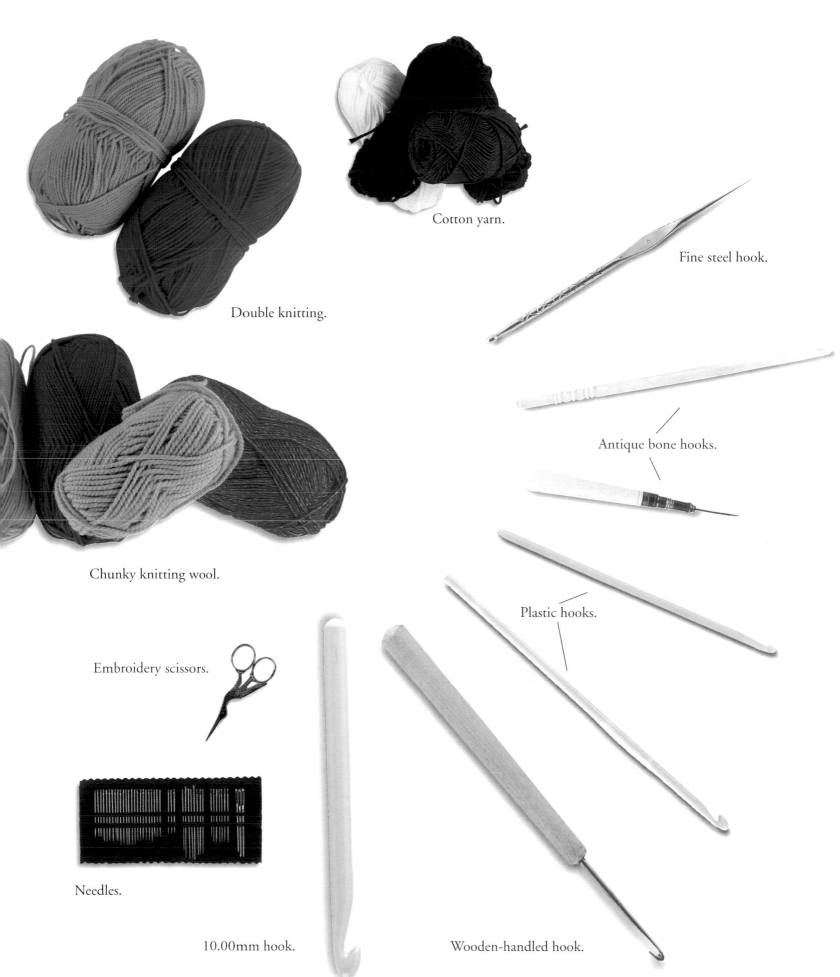

Cotton yarn.

Fine steel hook.

Double knitting.

Antique bone hooks.

Chunky knitting wool.

Plastic hooks.

Embroidery scissors.

Needles.

10.00mm hook.

Wooden-handled hook.

99

Starting Off

A crochet stitch is formed simply by using a hook to pull one loop of yarn through another. Unlike knitting, where there can be many stitches on the needles, there is only ever one single stitch on the hook, which makes it easy to manage. The thread and work are held in one hand, the hook in the other. As with any new skill, it will take practice to learn how to crochet with an even tension (gauge), but all workers evolve their own way of holding the yarn and hook. Take time to find the most natural movement – and try using a larger or smaller size hook to alter the tension (gauge). The hand positions should be reversed for left-handed workers; it may help to reflect the pictures in a small mirror.

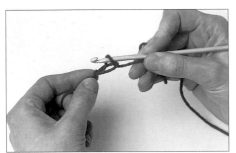

1 HOLDING THE HOOK AND MAKING THE LOOP Make a slip loop by wrapping the main yarn over the short end and using the hook to pull it through. Here the hook is held in the "pencil" position.

2 Tighten by pulling both ends of the yarn. Here the hook is in the "knife" position.

HOLDING THE YARN The work is held between the thumb and first finger of the left hand. To maintain a regular tension (gauge), the yarn is passed back over the two middle fingers, then under and round the little finger. This gives a taut length of thread between the first and second fingers, on which to work, while tension (gauge) is controlled with the tip of the second finger.

CHAIN STITCH (CH)

Chain is the basis for all crochet and the foundation on to which further stitches are worked.

1 Hold the slip loop firmly, then wrap the hook under and over the yarn (yoh or yo).

2 Carefully draw the yarn through the loop on the hook to form a new loop.

3 Repeat this process until the chain reaches the desired length.

FOLLOWING A PATTERN
All crochet instructions are written with special abbreviations and symbols to make them easy to understand. The most familiar are listed.

alt	alternate	inc	increase
beg	beginning	lp(s)	loop(s)
bet	between	patt (pat)	pattern
chs	chain	rep	repeat
	(chain stitches)	rnd	round
cont	continue	sc	single crochet
dc	double crochet	sk	skip
dec	decrease	sp(s)	space(s)
hdc	half double crochet	t-chs	turning chain
dtr	double treble	tog	together
	(triple)	tr	treble (triple)
htr	half treble (triple)	yoh (yo)	yarn over hook

* Instructions following an asterisk should be repeated as specified.
( ) Brackets either indicate a stitch combination which has to be repeated, or they enclose extra information such as the number of stitches made in a row.

CONVERSION CHART

UK	US
slip stitch (sl st)	slip stitch (sl st)
double crochet (dc)	single crochet (sc)
half treble (h tr)	half treble crochet (h dc)
treble (tr)	double crochet (dc)
double treble (d tr)	treble (tr)
triple treble (tr tr)	double treble (d tr)
work straight	work even
yarn over hook (yoh)	yarn over (yo)

Working in Stripes

Once the basic crochet stitches *(see page 199)* have been learnt, they can be combined to produce many interesting textures, but, with the imaginative use of colour, even simple rows of trebles can be transformed into striped or squared pattern swatches.

Checks and stripes are just some of the effects that can be created by combining colours.

1 HORIZONTAL STRIPES Stripes are created by working in bands of different colours. Join in the new yarn at the end of the previous row by using it to complete the last stitch.

2 The ends of the yarn can be cut off at the end of each stripe and joined back in when needed. The loose ends should then be sewn invisibly into the work.

3 Wider stripes are made by working two or more rows the same colour. When a repeating sequence is being used, carry the yarn loosely up the side of the work.

WORKING WITH TWO COLOURS

Diagonal or vertical stripes are worked by crocheting with two or more colours in each row. The same technique is used for blocks of colour, such as squares, and for more complicated intarsia patterns.

1 The colours are changed within a single row by swapping yarns over on the final stitch of each block. Draw the second colour through with the hook to complete the stitch.

2 Continue working along the row, changing colours every few stitches. The method is the same, whichever stitch is used.

3 Loose (floating) yarn is concealed by crocheting the next row of stitches over it when making narrow stripes; for wider three-coloured stripes, the yarn is carried across the back of the work.

Basic Stitches

There are five main crochet stitches from which all variations have developed. They progress from slip stitch, a travelling stitch which does not make any height, to tall double trebles (triples), depending on the number of loops from which they are formed. When working in rows, extra chain, called turning chain (t-ch) must be worked at the beginning of each row so that the yarn is at the right level to begin the next stitch. It is important to complete each row by working the last stitch into the turning chain of the previous row. This keeps the number of stitches constant and the sides straight. The first row of any stitch is worked through the back loop of the foundation chain, but on subsequent rows the hook passes under both loops of the previous stitch, from front to back, to give a firm fabric.

Clockwise from top: treble; half treble; double and crochet; double treble.

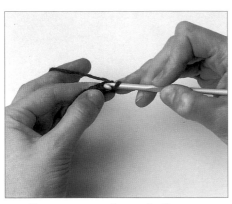

1 SLIP STITCH (SL ST) Skip 1ch, *insert hook under top lp of next ch.

2 Yoh (yo), draw through ch and lp on hook. (1sl st formed).

3 Repeat from * to end of ch. Turn, make 1 t-ch and cont, working the next sl st under both lps of 2nd st from hook. Work the last sl st of the row into the t-ch.

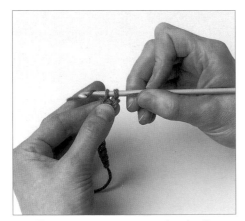

1 DOUBLE CROCHET (DC) Skip 1ch, * insert hook under top lp of next ch.

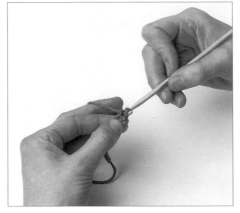

2 *Yoh, draw through ch only. Yoh and draw through both lps on hook (1dc formed). Repeat from * to end of ch. Turn.

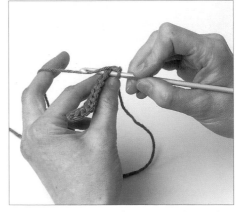

3 Make 1t-ch and cont, working the next dc under both lps of 2nd st from hook. Work the last dc of the row into the t-ch.

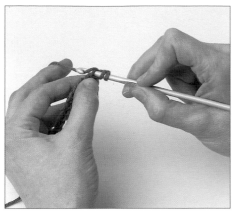

1 HALF TREBLE (HTR) Skip 2ch1 *yoh, insert hook under top lp of next ch.

2 Yoh, and draw through ch only (3lps on hook).

3 Yoh, draw through all 3lps on hook (1htr formed). Repeat from * to end of chain. Turn. Make 2t-ch and cont, working the next htr under both lps of the 2nd st from hook. Work the last htr of the row into the 2nd of 2t-ch of the previous row.

1 TREBLE (TR) Skip 3ch, *yoh, insert hook under top lp of next ch, yoh and draw yarn through ch only (3lps on hook).

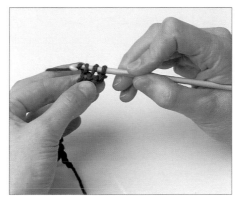

2 Yoh, draw through next 2lps on hook (2lps on hook).

3 Yoh, draw through 2 remaining lps on hook (1tr formed). Repeat from * to end of ch. Turn. Make 3t-ch and cont, working the next tr under both lps of the 2nd st from hook. Work the last tr of the row into the 3rd of 3t-ch of the previous row.

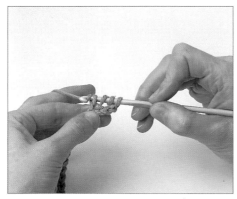

1 DOUBLE TREBLE (DTR) Skip 3ch, *yoh twice, insert hook under top lp of next ch, yoh and draw through ch (4lps on hook).

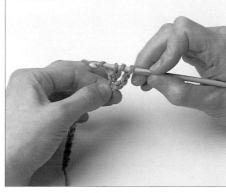

2 Yoh, draw through next 2lps on hook, (3lps on hook), yoh, draw through next 2lps on hook (2lps on hook).

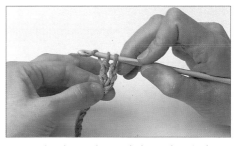

3 Yoh, draw through last 2lps (1dtr formed). Repeat from * to end. Turn. Make 4 t-ch and cont, working the next dtr under both lps of 2nd st from hook. Work the last dtr of the row into the 4th of 4t-ch of the previous row.

FINISHING OFF

All work should be finished off properly to prevent it unravelling. After the last stitch, pull the final loop out with the hook, and cut the yarn, leaving an end of about 25cm (5in). This loose end can then be sewn invisibly into the work using a tapestry needle.

Working in the Round

When crocheting in the round, the foundation chain is joined to make a loop. The stitches are then worked into this ring, in ever-increasing circles, without turning. This technique is used to make small medallions and motifs which can be joined together patchwork-style, as well as traditional lace doilies and larger accessories such as shawls or tablecloths. Hats and other three-dimensional items can be created by increasing and decreasing the number of stitches in each round.

Left: Small floral shapes are easy to crochet in the round. These flowers are joined together by the edges of their petals.

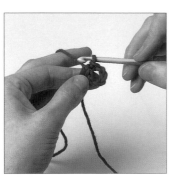

1 MAKING THE FOUNDATION RING
Make a short length of chain stitch and insert the hook under the top loop of the last stitch.

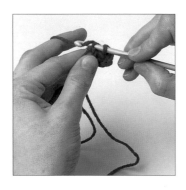

2 Join by pulling the yarn through the loop to form a slip stitch.

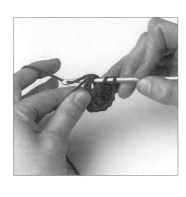

3 Work the first round into the ring, so that the hook actually passes through it to pick up the yarn.

TREBLE (TRIPLE) CIRCLES
Circles of crochet can be made by increasing the number of stitches in alternate rounds. New colours can be joined on each round and the ends concealed by working over them. Each round starts with one, two or three standing chain, which take the place of the first stitch, in the same way as turning chain.

1 **Round 1** Make 5ch and join with sl st into 1st ch. 3ch, then work 16tr into ring. Join with a sl st to 3rd ch st. **Round 2** 3ch, 1tr into same sp as tr, (2tr into 1tr) to end of round. Join with a sl st to 3rd ch st.

2 **Round 3** 3ch, (2tr into 1tr, 1tr into 1tr) to end of round. Join with a sl st to 3rd ch st. **Round 4** Work (2tr into 1tr, 2tr into 2tr). **Round 5** (2tr into 1tr, 3 tr into 3tr).

Right: This sunflower is an introduction to working with clusters of stitches, a common way of shaping within a circle. Here they are formed from triple trebles (triples), abbreviated as tr tr.

INSTRUCTIONS

Make 8ch and join with a sl st.

Round 1 3ch, 15tr into ring, join with sl st to 3rd ch.

Round 2 Sl st into sp between next 2tr. 2dc into 5p. 2dc into each sp to end, sl to 1st dc (32dcs). Join next colour.

MAKING THE CLUSTER

Round 3 6ch, * yoh (yo) 3 times, insert hook into next dc. Yoh (yo) and draw through (5lps on hook), (yoh (yo) and draw through 2lps) twice, (2lps on hook). Repeat from * twice, yoh (yo) and through all 4lps to form cluster. ** 9ch

(4tr tr into next 4dc to make cluster). Repeat from ** to end of round, sl st to top of 1st cluster.

Round 5 1ch (9dc over 9ch) to end of round. Join with a sl st to 1ch, finish off.

Right: These Irish crochet roses are worked in the round, using a thick Aran wool. They have been appliquéd on to a richly cabled knitted background.

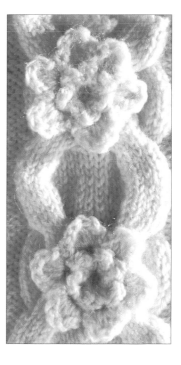

Left: These hexagons are worked from remnants of bright yarn. The stained-glass window effect comes from edging each motif with black, which contrasts dramatically with the other colours.

Crochet Squares

The familiar afghan, or grannie squares, are long-established favourites. The first afghan rugs were made as a means of economizing; at one time yarn was precious and outgrown garments would be unravelled so that the yarn could be re-used. Crochet squares were a practical way of keeping warm, and as a planned colour scheme was then a luxury, colours were used at random. Today, afghan square rugs are still a good way of using up odd balls of yarn, for beginners and experienced workers alike.

Above: This sampler combines afghan square techniques with Irish crochet roses and clusters. It is worked in cotton yarn for a crisp texture.

THE BASIC SQUARE

The squares can be made to any size; small multicoloured arrangements have a jewel-like effect, particularly if edged with a single colour, or one single huge square can make a useful blanket.

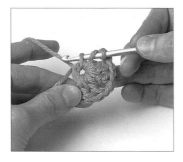

1 Make 6ch and join with sl st to form foundation ring.
Round 1 3ch (to stand as 1st tr), then 2tr into the ring, (* 2ch, 3tr) 3 times, 2ch, join with sl st to 3rd ch. Finish off 1st colour.

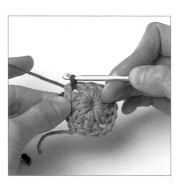

2 Join 2nd colour to one corner by holding the end of the yarn and pulling a loop under the chain. Work the first stitches over the loose ends of both colours.

3 **Round 2** 3ch, (2tr, 2ch, 3tr) into same space, (3tr, 2ch, 3tr into next sp) 3 times, join with sl st to top of 3ch. Continue the following rounds in the same way, working a 3-tr cluster into every space along the four sides, with two in each corner.

JOINING MOTIFS

Individual squares can be joined together in two ways, by sewing or with double crochet. Hand stitching gives a flat seam, which is invisible if worked in matching yarn, while crocheting produces a ridged effect. All the ends should be darned in securely.

1 Thread a tapestry needle with a 45cm (18in) length of yarn. Fasten on with a back stitch, concealing the end. Hold the squares, with wrong sides facing, and stitch firmly through both loops on each side.

2 Double crochet makes a strong, attractive join, worked through both loops on each side. Squares can be joined singly, or when all the motifs for one project have been completed. Lay them out in the final order, then work all the horizontal, then all the vertical joins.

Left: The centre of this afghan variation is made from eight raised clusters. The combination of chenille and woollen yarns gives an interesting effect.

Left: Hexagonal afghan motifs can be made by working 12 stitches into the first round, two to a side, and increasing in the usual way.

Left: Many variations on the basic square can be worked by mixing the colours within each round. A patchwork block effect can be created by choosing a predominant background colour such as cream, and keeping to a tight colour scheme.

SHELLS AND CLUSTERS

Shells are fan-shaped groups of stitches made by working several trebles into one space. Clusters appear as inverted fans, and are created by retaining the final loops of several adjacent trebles on the hook while they are worked, then drawing them together with one movement. By combining the two, many interesting patterns can be created.

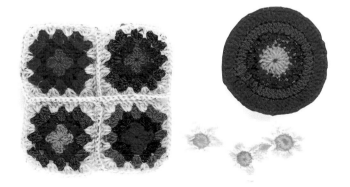

WORKING A SHELL
Insert the hook into the 3rd ch from hook, then work 7tr into this sp. Anchor final st with a sl st into 3rd ch from hook.

Above: These coloured swatches illustrate just a few of the textured crochet fabrics that can be developed by working alternate rows of shells and clusters.

Filet Crochet

Filet crochet is an old technique, which reached elaborate heights in the late nineteenth century. It is still very popular today, particularly in Holland, France and Germany, where it is used to make curtains, tablecloths and figurative panels, as well as decorative edgings. It consists of a regular square mesh, made from trebles (triples) and chain stitches, and the design is created by filling in some of the spaces with blocks of stitches.

This flower basket design was adapted from a pattern that first appeared in the 1900s, when many women led a more leisurely life and had time to work exquisite crochet to show off their skills. It uses a fine thread worked with a steel hook.

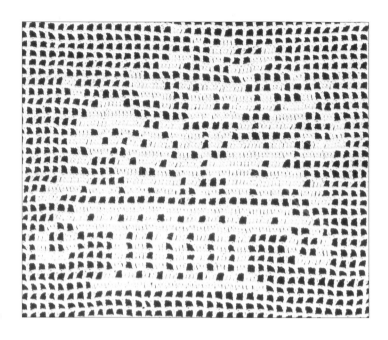

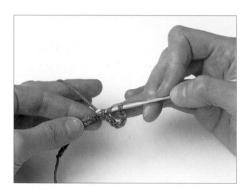

1 MAKING THE MESH Each charted square represents 3ch, so calculate the length of the foundation chain by multiplying the number of squares needed by 3 and adding 5t-ch. Work 1tr into the 8th ch from hook.

2 (Make 2ch, skip 2ch, 1tr into next ch) to end of row, ending with 1tr, 5t-ch.

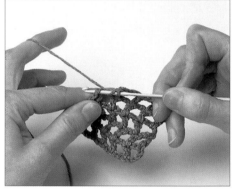

3 For the next and following rows, * 1tr into 2nd tr from hook, skip 2ch, 1tr into next tr, to end, 5t-ch. Work the trs through both lps of the previous tr.

1 MAKING THE BLOCKS A block is made by working 2tr *under* the 2ch of the previous row. For a block at the beginning of a row, make 3t-ch then make 2tr into 2ch 5p, and 1tr into next tr.

2 A checkerboard effect can be built up by working alternate blocks and spaces. Work the last tr into the t-ch of previous row.

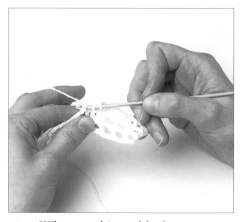

3 When working a block on top of another block, make the 4tr through both loops of the previous stitches.

FOLLOWING A PATTERN

There are many publications which include filet crochet patterns. They are printed on a square grid and are easy to follow. Each plain square represents a mesh and each filled-in square is a block. The first and following odd rows are worked from right to left, starting at the bottom right square, and the even rows read from left to right. For complicated designs, it is worth making an enlarged photocopy of the chart and marking off the lines as they are completed to keep track of how the work is progressing. Many cross stitch patterns can be adapted to filet crochet, and it is easy to draw up designs on to squared paper.

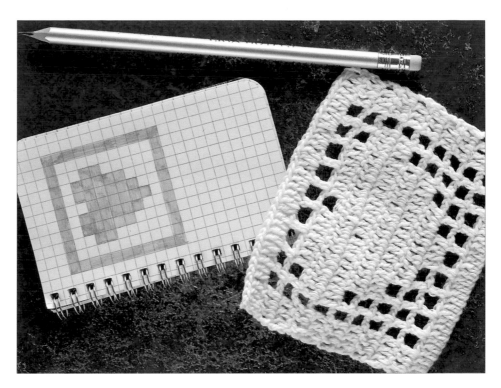

Filet crochet can be worked on a large or small scale, and in a variety of threads. Extra decoration has been added to this simple indigo cotton mesh by interweaving the trebles (triples) with striped braid. This technique would work well on lacy garments, which could be decorated with silk ribbons.

Although not strictly filet crochet, this chenille scarf is worked in a V-shaped mesh variation, which gives it an interesting texture.

Special Techniques

T his section is an introduction to the many needlework techniques which fall outside the usual categories. Some, like smocking and rug-making, are crafts in themselves, whilst others will provide innovative ideas to add an individual touch to your projects. Familiar items such as beads, sequins, tassels, ribbons and buttons can all be used in creative and sometimes unexpected ways – all that is needed is a little ingenuity!

Dyeing

Using dyes to bring original colours to yarn and cloth can add a whole new dimension to many textile crafts. Traditional vegetable dyeing techniques give subtle and sometimes unexpected hues, and using them is an art in itself. Chemical dyes, however, are straightforward and quick to use, and are available in both hot- and cold-water versions for synthetic and natural fibres. Special compounds that can be used safely in the washing machine are suitable for larger quantities of material.

SPACE-DYED YARNS

Hanks of cotton thread or pure wool can be dyed as easily as fabrics, with exciting results. The random colour bands that are formed by space-dyeing yarn will create interesting patterns when the threads are worked up. Finer threads can be dyed for free-form embroidery stitches, in specially chosen co-ordinating colours.

1 Wind the yarn into hanks and secure at intervals. Loose ties will allow the colours to blend gently; tight ties will leave a resist band of white yarn. Soak well, then wring out excess water.

2 Following the manufacturer's instructions, prepare the hot-water dye solution in an old saucepan and maintain it at simmering point. When working with several dyes, only a small amount of each powder need be used. Holding the yarn with a pair of tongs, dip the parts of the skein in between the ties into the dye for a minute. Repeat with the second and third colours.

3 Wash the skeins in a hand-wash liquid to remove any surplus dye, rinse well and allow to dry thoroughly. Carefully snip away the ties without cutting through the yarn, then wind into balls.

It is fascinating to knit or crochet with space-dyed yarns and watch the haphazard colours fall into orderly diamonds and stripes.

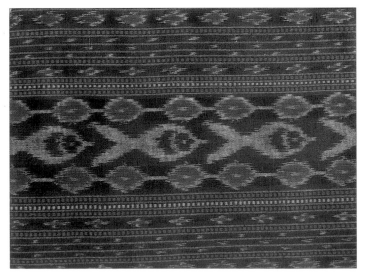

Carefully planned space-dyeing is used to produce the figurative and geometric design that patterns the warp of this decorative Ikat fabric.

Tie-Dye Scarf

Tie-dyeing is a well-known way of producing surface patterns on fabric or garments, and, perhaps because of this overfamiliarity, it is often underestimated. Simply knotting, gathering, folding or pleating the material and tying it with string, or binding it with elastic bands, will create varied and unpredictable shapes. Several colours can be used on one piece for a vivid multicoloured effect.

MATERIALS
Large scarf in plain white silk or cotton
String
Hot- or cold-water dye
Salt

VARIATION 1
Circular designs are created by placing a bead or button in the centre of the fabric and holding it in place with an elastic band. Bunch the rest of the material together and tie it at intervals with string.

VARIATION 2
Roll or fold the fabric into a roll and bind at random for a striped effect.

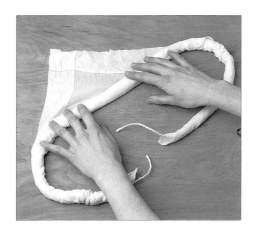

1 If the scarf is new, wash it to remove any dressing (finishing). Rinse well, then wring out. Lay it out on a flat surface and place a long piece of string over one corner. Carefully roll the fabric over the string.

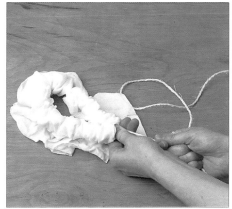

2 Pull the two ends of the string together, gently easing the fabric into a circular shape and making sure that it does not unravel. Knot the string securely.

3 Dye the scarf, following the manufacturer's instructions, and using an old saucepan as a dyebath. Cut the string and unroll the fabric. Wash again to remove any surplus dye.

Fabric-Strip Rugs

A hand-made hearth rug in front of the fireplace has long been a feature of family life. Scraps of wool and fabric can be stitched or tufted on to a backing cloth or canvas to form elaborate pictorial designs, but the quickest rugmaking methods are those in which the rug itself is constructed from strips of braided fabric.

BRAIDED RUGS

Braided rugs, which are made from a coiled stitched braid of material, are among some of the oldest surviving antique examples. This technique was often used in combination with knitting, particularly by the Amish people of Lancaster County, Pennsylvania. A central medallion, made from fabric knitted into squares or six-pointed stars, would be surrounded by braided bands. If possible, cut the fabric strips on the diagonal so they will be less rigid. Cloth salvaged from women's and girls' dresses was cut into long strips, then joined and wound into a ball for working. Knitting with fabric strips can be hard work since they have no elasticity. It is important to keep the tension quite loose and to work on extra-large needles – size 10.00mm upwards.

1 MAKING A KNITTED RUG Collect together scraps and remnants of patterned dress-weight fabrics and tear into 4cm (1½in) strips. Sew together and wind into a ball.

2 The rug is knitted in strips of approximately 7.5cm (3in) wide, as anything else would be too unwieldy. Cast on 10 stitches and work in garter stitch as usual. This will make the rug reversible.

3 The finished strips can be sewn together with strong thread. By working in strips of even length, you can produce a chequered pattern.

This crochet rug has been worked in basic double crochet stitch with a 12.00mm hook. Each round is worked in a separate colour to give a pattern of concentric circles and the soft colours come from using old fabric.

Braided Rug

The first fabric-strip floorcoverings were made at a time when new cloth was in short supply. Their distinctive muted appearance came from the use of mixed fabrics, recycled from clothing and domestic textiles, as few of the early makers could afford the luxury of planning a special colour scheme for their work. The striking effect of this round rug shows how a traditional technique can be updated to create an unquestionably modern effect. It is made from a vivid selection of bright acetate fabrics, overdyed ginghams and sari fabric.

MATERIALS
Selection of coloured fabrics
Button-hole thread
Sewing needle
Safety pin
Kitchen weights (optional)
Heavy-duty fabric for the backing (optional)

1 Tear the fabric, along the grain, into strips that measure about 6.5m (2½in) wide. Three strips of the same shade braided together will give a broad strip of colour, whereas mixing the colours will produce a "speckled" effect.

2 Stitch three strips together at one end, then secure to a firm surface: fasten to the arm of an upholstered chair with a safety pin; hold down with large kitchen weights, or attach to a wall hook.

3 Plait (braid) the three strips together, turning the raw edges to the inside. Further lengths can either be stitched on, end to end, as the plait progresses, or folded around the end of the preceding strip as shown, to save time sewing.

4 When the braid is a few metres (yards) long, the sewing process can begin. Tidy the stitched end, then, working on a flat surface, coil the braid around it. Sew together with ladder stitch or a flat stitch, catching together a small amount of fabric from each side, and turning to maintain a round shape. A strip of about 18m (20yd) will make a circle of 60cm (24in) diameter, and the rug can be enlarged to any size. A heavy-duty backing fabric can be sewn on if the rug is to receive a lot of wear.

Smocking

Smocking has been used in garment making, as an ornamental method of gathering surplus material, since medieval times. In the English countryside, smock frocks were worn by male agricultural workers for centuries and the tradition survived in rural Essex among the older generation until the 1930s. The smock was a practical, protective, outer garment made from tough linen that could stand up to heavy wear and repel water. It was made from large rectangles of fabric with the fullness gathered into narrow pleats at the yoke, shoulders and cuffs and held together with rows of smocking stitches.

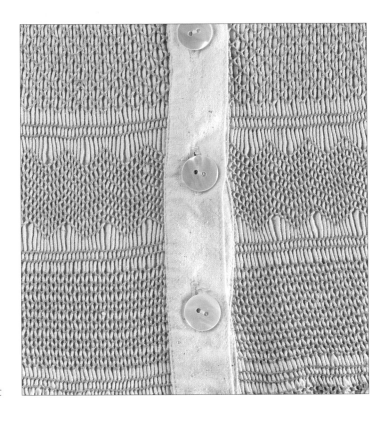

HOW TO WORK SMOCKING
Before being embroidered, the fabric must be drawn into narrow tubes. Rows of dots, in a grid formation, are marked on the reverse of the fabric. Iron-on transfers are the quickest way to prepare plain or patterned fabric.

1 Place the transfer face down and press carefully. Work a row of gathering stitches from right to left, along each horizontal line, picking up a few threads at each dot.

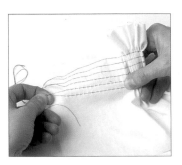

2 Pull all the lengths of cotton up evenly, so that the fabric falls into a series of tubes. Secure the ends by tying them.

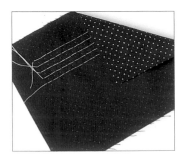

3 You can gather fabrics printed with regular dots or checks by simply following the lines of the pattern.

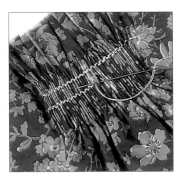

HONEYCOMB STITCH
This is worked along two rows of dots. Bring the needle out to the left of the first fold and work two back stitches over the first two folds. Bring the needle down and out on the next row of dots, between the next two folds. Work two back stitches over these and bring the needle back up to the top line of stitches. Continue to the end of the row, then work the next line of stitches on the third and fourth rows of dots. Surface honeycomb stitch is worked in the same way, but the needle is passed over the surface of the fabric, rather than through the tube.

CABLE STITCH
This stitch is also worked from left to right. Start at the left of the first fold. Be sure that the thread lies below the needle. Make a stitch over the second fold and bring the needle out between the first two folds. Hold the thread above the needle and make a stitch over the third fold, bringing the needle out between the second and third fold. Continue to the end.

Child's Sun Dress

The appealing charm of smocking has made it a favourite for children's clothes, and generations of young girls have worn floral print frocks with smocked yokes. This pretty sun dress would fit a toddler of up to eighteen months, and requires only the most basic of dressmaking skills. The bodice is worked in honeycomb stitch, which produces a very elastic fabric that eliminates the need for a back opening or any fastening.

MATERIALS
35 x 154cm (14 x 60in) piece of dotted cotton fabric
Matching cotton sewing thread; sewing machine
Cotton tacking (basting) thread; needle; dressmaker's pins
Stranded embroidery thread in blue, blue-green,
green, pale blue-green, white, pale lime green,
yellow and bright yellow

1 Cut a strip of fabric measuring 30 x 154cm (12 x 60in). Turn in a narrow hem at the top and bottom edges, machine stitch and trim back. Turn over and machine again.

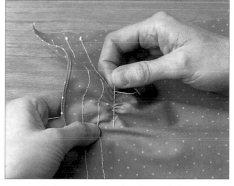

2 On the wrong side of the fabric, work six long rows of contrasting gathering thread, starting about 2cm (¾in) in from one hemmed edge. Use the printed dots as a guide, but if they are too far apart, pick up a few threads of cloth between each one.

3 Draw up the gathers and secure by wrapping thread round pins. On the right side of the fabric, beginning at the outside edge of the gathers, work eight rows of surface honey-comb stitch in colours as follows: blue, blue-green, green, pale blue-green, white, pale lime green, yellow and bright yellow. Remove the gathering stitches and machine stitch the back seam. Tidy with zigzag stitch and trim.

4 Cut four strips of fabric each measuring 5 x 30cm (2 x 12in) to make the straps. Fold with right sides together and machine stitch, tapering off at one end. Trim and turn through. Press, top stitch and tidy the raw end. Sew the straps securely to the inside of the yoke at the top of the stitching. Finish off by knotting together at the shoulders.

Ribbons and Bows

There are many craft applications for ribbons, which are available in an ever-increasing choice of weights, patterns and widths. Manufacturers are constantly developing new ideas, such as sheer rainbow gauzes, metallic gold and silver braids (which are ideal for Christmas decorations) and reversible printed satin ribbons. More traditional types – moiré taffeta, country-style ginghams, luxurious velvets and grosgrain – can be found in a wide range of colours in craft shops and department stores.

RIBBON ROSES, ROSETTES, BOWS AND FAVOURS

These can be used to add a personal touch to all kinds of gifts and accessories. Special Valentine ribbons printed with hearts, Christmas designs or wedding ribbons with a pattern of bells and lucky horseshoes can all be used to decorate special presents. Look out for pastel baby ribbons to decorate tiny garments or blankets. Lengths of ribbon can also be appliquéd on to a fabric background.

Ribbon roses are suprisingly straightforward to make and can be used to decorate many different sewing projects. Satin ribbons give a luxurious effect, especially if several harmonizing colours are used together.

1 RIBBON ROSE
Fold the ribbon under at a right angle, two-thirds along its length, and then pass the long end under the triangular fold and hold in place. Pass the short end under, then continue to make accordion folds to the end of the ribbon.

2 Hold the two ends together and grip with the thumb and forefinger of one hand while drawing up the long end. This action ruffles the ribbon and forms the rose.

3 Still holding the rose, so that it does not come undone, stitch through the base to hold the petals in place.

WIRE-EDGED RIBBONS
These make spectacular bows, which will retain their shape. The loops and ends can be gently bent into flowing curves.

Ribbon-Weave Cushion (Pillow)

Authentic tartan (plaid) and textured grosgrain ribbons are woven together to make this eye-catching cushion (pillow). The basic technique used is called a square (or tabby) weave. The foundation ribbons are laid down to form the warp, then further lengths of ribbon, known as the weft, are passed alternately under and over them. Endless variations can be produced, by using different colours and widths of ribbon in various combinations.

Materials

122cm (48in) length of tartan (plaid) ribbon in each of the following:
  4cm (1½in) red; 2cm (¾in) blue
122cm (48in) length of plain ribbon in each of the following:
  6mm (¼in) green; 6mm (¼in) red
  6mm (¼in) blue
60cm (24in) length of 15mm (⅝in) yellow ribbon
Drawing board or large piece of cardboard
Masking tape
35cm (14in) square of iron-on fusible bonding
Sewing machine; matching machine sewing thread
Dressmaker's pins
35cm (14in) square of backing fabric
30cm (12in) cushion (pillow) pad

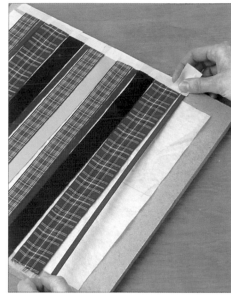

1 Cut the ribbon into 35cm (14in) lengths. Working on a drawing board or piece of cardboard, arrange as shown to form the warp and secure each piece with masking tape. Place the fusible bonding underneath the ribbon, adhesive side upwards.

2 Form the ribbon weave by interlacing the rest of the ribbon with the weft. Fix each length down on the right-hand side, pass it alternately above and below the other ribbons, then tape it down at the left. Gently ease each ribbon into place, pushing it against the preceding one, for a regular appearance.

3 Fix the bonding into place with a warm iron and damp cloth, to hold the ribbons together. Machine stitch round the outside edge, then remove the masking tape. With right sides together, pin and stitch the backing fabric to the ribbon weave, leaving a 2.5cm (1in) seam allowance. Trim, clip the corners and turn through. Insert the cushion pad and slip stitch the fourth side closed.

Tassels and Pompoms

A whole art surrounds the making of furnishing trimmings, which is correctly known as *passementerie*, and the most elaborate tassels and fringes can be very expensive. The basic shapes are not difficult to make, however, and a special tassel can add a distinctive finishing touch to many projects. Virtually any yarn or thread can be used: raffia gives a natural feel to bedroom and bathroom accessories, gold machine embroidery thread is extravagant enough for the most special gifts, chenille yarn is luxurious, while bright wools or cotton yarns create a less sophisticated effect. Tassels can be made to coordinate with any interior design scheme and to adorn most soft furnishings.

HOW TO MAKE A TASSEL

Different weights of yarn will produce different results, but the basic method does not vary. The top of the tassel can be further ornamented with a binding of contrasting threads or by the addition of beads.

1 Cut a piece of cardboard slightly wider than the finished tassel and wind the thread around it. Tie a length of thread around the loop when it has reached the required thickness.

2 Slip the loop from the cardboard, hold the tied end firmly and cut through the threads at the opposite end.

3 Keep the tassel in shape by binding the top with matching thread and finishing off the ends securely.

BLACK VELVET AND CHENILLE YARN

Opulent velvet and chenille yarn have been combined to make this spectacular cushion (pillow) above. The blue tassels are sewn by hand at regular intervals and contrast with the smooth texture of the velvet cover.

Pompom Necklace

Like tassels, pompoms are easy and fun to make, especially for children. They can be used to decorate hats, scarves and sweaters, strung together to make soft toys – caterpillars or snakes – or threaded with beads to make this colourful play necklace. These pompoms are all made from a single colour of cotton yarn, which has a rich velvety finish, but interesting multicoloured effects can be produced by mixing yarns.

MATERIALS
Pair of compasses; pencil
Cardboard
Darning needle
Remnants of cotton yarn in various colours
Round cord elastic
Multicoloured wooden beads

1 Using the compasses, draw two 4cm (1½in) circles on the cardboard and mark 2cm (¾in) circles within them. Cut out round the outer card and inner circles to form the two cardboard rings. Thread the darning needle with yarn and, holding the two cardboard rings together, begin to wrap the yarn around the cardboard as shown.

2 Continue until the cardboard is completely covered and the centre space filled, adding extra yarn as necessary. Cut carefully around the outside edge, inserting the scissor blades between the discs.

3 Wrap a length of yarn several times around the cut strands, and between the cardboard discs. Tie loosely in a knot, then remove the cardboard discs. Trim the pompom to make a tidy round ball. Make seven more pompoms in the same way, using different colours.

4 Thread the needle with elastic and string on three wooden beads. Push the needle through the centre of the first pompom, then add another three beads.

Continue until all the elements have been threaded together, then tie the elastic tightly in a knot and hide the ends by threading them back through the beads.

Beads and Sequins

Embroidery with beads and sequins has always been associated with glamorous fashion garments – from the fantasy wedding dresses that provide the finale to Paris fashion shows, to the eleborate confections worn by ballroom dancers. A more restrained use of beading can bring interest to many textile techniques, by highlighting detail and adding colour.

WORKING WITH BEADS AND SEQUINS

Sequins can be bought from many craft suppliers. Some of the most exciting varieties are imported from India and come in exotic shapes and colours. They can be sewn on in three ways: in overlapping rows so that the thread is hidden; with decorative contrasting stitches; or anchored in place with a small bead.

FLOWER SEQUINS
Tiny white rocaille beads will make attractive ornamental centres for these flower-shaped sequins.

SEWING A ROW OF SEQUINS
Bring the needle through a sequin's centre hole and make a straight stitch over the edge. Place the edge of the next sequin over the hole in the first. Bring the needle up through its centre and sew down, over the edge.

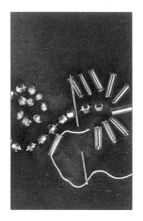

SEWING ON BEADS
Individual beads can be sewn into elaborate patterns: stitch each one down with a fine needle.

CONTINUOUS THREAD
Using decorative back stitches, so that the thread can be seen through the fabric, gold sequins have been sewn on to metallic organza (organdy).

FLAT SEQUINS
Using a fine needle, thread through both the sequin and a bead, then take the thread back through the hole so that the sequin is held in place by the bead.

CUP SEQUINS
This star-shaped Indian Christmas decoration is covered in glittering muticoloured cup sequins, held down by small iridescent beads.

Lace edgings can be decorated with beads and sequins to emphasize aspects of the woven design.

Once part of a chair seat cover, this hydrangea-like flower is made up entirely of beads that have been stitched on to double-thread canvas.

Beaded Heart

Silk flowers and fine satin ribbons combine with beads and sequins to lend an Edwardian appearance to this romantic heart. It is based on a piece of antique lace that has been given a new lease of life: the damaged areas have been disguised with cut-out motifs and beading, and the fragile fabric tacked (basted) on to a heart-shaped padded cushion (pillow) as support. The finished heart would look lovely on a dressing-table, but could also be hung in a wardrobe to perfume clothes.

MATERIALS
Satin fabric
Matching sewing thread
Polyester toy stuffing
Potpourri (optional)
Fragment of old lace
Tiny glass beads
Translucent sequins
Dressmaker's pins
Silk flowers and leaves
Narrow ribbon

1 Cut out two heart shapes from the satin and, with right sides facing, stitch together, leaving a small space in one side. Clip the curves and corners and turn through. Fill with toy stuffing and slip stitch the opening together. Potpourri could be added to give a sweet scent.

2 Mark out the heart shape on the lace, then sew it with beads and sequins, picking out the shapes within the lace pattern. Cut out small motifs from the spare pieces of lace to cover any holes.

3 Pin the lace on to the heart cushion (pillow), stretching it over the upper part and folding over the surplus fabric. Stitch in place, then sew on a posy of silk flowers and ribbons.

123

Buttons

Buttons are essentially a utilitarian part of everyday life, used by everybody to do up their clothing. Over the years they have been made from every imaginable material: horn, seashell, coconut, plastic, glass, pottery and metal. Elaborate buttons have always been a fashion accessory in themselves. Eighteenth-century dandies sported buttons of gold set with semi-precious stones or even painted with miniature portraits. Today the interlocking Cs on a Chanel suit are instantly recognizable and say as much about the wearer as monogrammed blazer buttons.

SELF-COVER BUTTONS

Fabric-covered buttons are used by dressmakers as an unobtrusive yet decorative fastening. Larger version are used for soft furnishings to match or contrast with upholstery fabric, but can also be covered with small circles of embroidery or needlepoint.

This fascinating set of buttons was made as showcase for various specialized stitches and includes blackwork, drawn threadwork, needleweaving, laid threadwork and inlay appliqué.

1 Following the manufacturer's guide, which is supplied with self-cover button kit, cut out a circle of fabric to fit the button top.

2 Run a gathering thread around the edge of the fabric, draw up and slip over the button top. Pull tightly and secure, then press the backing firmly onto place.

Buttons can be combined with many embroidery and applique techniques. Mother-of-pearl shirt buttons have been stitched to the centres of these cotton flowers and are well suited to the naive graphic style of the piece.

Button Mirror

In addition to their obvious function, buttons can be put to many decorative uses. This mirror frame is ornamented with simple embroidery stitches, tiny discs of Indian shisha glass and round mother-of-pearl buttons. Raid the button box to find a selection of buttons in various shapes, colours and sizes; this monochrome colour scheme is just one interpretation of the idea.

MATERIALS

Dressmaker's chalk or carbon
Piece of black cotton twill 5cm (2in)
*   larger all round than the frame*
Wooden frame 5cm (2in) wide
Mother-of-pearl buttons
Embroidery thread in red and silver
Shisha glass
Pva adhesive
Buttonhole thread
Mirror to fit inside the frame
Panel pins

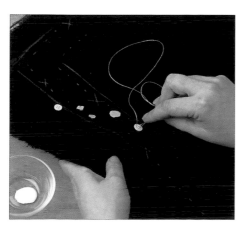

1 Draw the outline on to the fabric, using the frame as a template. Mark on the positions of the two rows of shisha glass, buttons and crosses. Sew on the buttons, using red or silver thread, and glue on the shisha glass with pva adhesive.

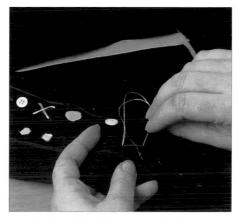

2 Embroider the crosses in silver thread. The arrangement of shisha, buttons and crosses should not be too orderly or regular. Cut out the centre rectangle of fabric, leaving an allowance of at least 2.5cm (1in).

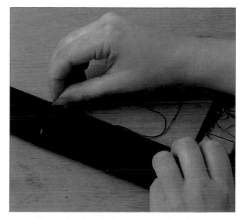

3 Stretch the fabric over the frame and fold over the edges. Draw together with large stitches in buttonhole thread. Mitre the outside corners and neatly finish the inside corners. Fix the mirror securely in place with panel pins.

Glossary

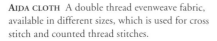

AIDA CLOTH A double thread evenweave fabric, available in different sizes, which is used for cross stitch and counted thread stitches.

ANTI-FRAYING SOLUTION A proprietary liquid, available from department stores and haberdashers, which is applied to fabric to prevent cut edges from unravelling.

APPLIQUÉ An ornamental sewing technique, in which cut-out pieces of one fabric are sewn on to a contrasting background to form a design.

BASTING (SEE TACKING)

BATIK A resist method of patterning fabric, in which the areas not being dyed are covered with wax.

BATTING (SEE WADDING)

BEESWAX A solid block of natural beeswax is used to strengthen sewing or quilting thread and to prevent it fraying during work.

BIAS BINDING A strip of material cut on the bias, or cross grain, which is used to bind hems or for decoration.

BLOCKING Diagonally worked needlepoint stitches tend to distort the canvas, so the finished piece has to be damp stretched, or blocked, to restore the original shape.

BOBBIN The spool which holds the lower thread on a sewing machine. The tension can be altered by adjusting the screw on the bobbin case.

BOLSTER A long, cylindrical pillow or cushion.

BROCADE A rich, woven furnishing fabric with a raised design.

BRODERIE ANGLAISE A white cotton lace with machine embroidered decoration.

BUTT To join two ends together without overlapping them.

CALICO A white or unbleached coarse cotton fabric.

CHAMBRAY A woven cotton fabric with a white weft and a coloured warp, often used to make shirts.

CHECKERBOARD A pattern made up of alternate light and dark squares, resembling a chess board.

CHENILLE A textured, velvet-like yarn, originally used for embroidery, but now usually knitted. A chenille needle is thick, with a large eye and a sharp point.

COTTON LAWN A fine dress-making weight pure cotton fabric, often printed with floral patterns.

CREWEL Crewel work is a form of embroidery worked in a fine 2-ply wool (crewel wool) on linen, which was popular in the seventeenth century. The designs were based on natural imagery of plants, fruit and flowers. A crewel needle is sharp, with a long, easily threaded eye.

DÉCOUPAGE A method of decorating objects by sticking down cut-out shapes or pictorial motifs.

DENIM A hard-wearing twill (drill) cotton fabric.

DOUBLE KNITTING YARN A 4-ply wool, also known as knitting worsted.

DRESSMAKER'S CHALK Traditional tailor's chalk, in block or pencil form, is used to transfer designs or pattern marking to fabric. The marks can easily be brushed away.

DRESSMAKER'S FADING PEN Also called a quilting pen, this special felt-tip is used to draw designs directly on to fabric. Any marks made will fade completely within a few days. Water-erasable versions are also available.

EMBROIDERY HOOP A hoop, or tambour frame, consists of two wooden rings between which a piece of fabric is stretched, to produce a taut surface for embroidery.

FEED DOG The part of a sewing machine that feeds the fabric under the needle and presser foot to ensure a regular stitch. It is lowered for free machine embroidery.

FAIR ISLE A multicoloured style of knitting which originated in the Shetland Isles and which consists of intricate horizontal bands of pattern.

FOUR-SQUARE BLOCK Many traditional patchwork patterns are based on the subdivision of a square made up of four rows of four smaller squares.

FREEHAND STITCHING Machine or hand embroidery which is worked freely across the fabric surface, rather than over a given outline.

GAUGE (SEE TENSION)

GINGHAM A two-coloured woven checked fabric.

GROSGRAIN A heavy silk or rayon ribbon, woven with a textured rib.

GUIPURE LACE A machine-made lace in which the individual pattern motifs are joined by threads, rather than woven into a supporting net.

HABUTAI SILK A fine Chinese silk, available in many colours, often used for lining.

HANK A loop or skein of yarn or thread.

IKAT FABRIC A woven fabric on which the pattern has been formed by dying particular areas of the warp threads.

IMAGE TRANSFER SOLUTION A proprietary liquid, which is used to transfer a printed image from paper to fabric.

INDELIBLE FELT-TIP PEN A permanent marker pen, used for marking designs when the backing fabric will be covered completely with stitches, e.g. for tracing needlepoint designs on to canvas.

INTARSIA A knitting technique in which a multicoloured motif is worked on a plain background, also known as Jacquard.

IRON-ON FUSIBLE BONDING A paper-backed adhesive web, which is used for bonding two layers of fabric.

IRON-ON WADDING (BATTING) A bonded polyester fibre, with heat-activated adhesive on one side, used mainly for quilting.

ISOMETRIC GRAPH PAPER A type of graph paper used by architects, which is based on a grid made up of equilateral triangles, rather than squares.

LAMETTA Metallic foil strings or strips used for Christmas and other decorations.

LANOLIN The natural protective waterproofing found in sheep's wool.

LUREX The trade name for a fine glittering, metallic thread, or any fabric woven or knitted from the thread.

MITRE The method of finishing corners without overlapping the fold or seam.

MOIRÉ TAFFETA A watermarked woven silk.

MOTIF A design element which is repeated to form a pattern, or used singly.

MOUNTING BOARD (MAT) A versatile, medium-weight card-board, available in many colours, used in picture framing.

ORGANZA (ORGANDY) A fine, crisp fabric woven from silk or man-made fibres.

PERCALE A closely woven cotton fabric, which is often used for bed linen.

PERLE COTTON A lustrous twisted thread, available in several thicknesses, which is used for embroidery and crochet.

PERSIAN WOOL A woollen yarn, consisting of three separable strands, used for embroidery and needlepoint.

QUILTER'S SQUARE A clear plastic square marked with regular lines, used to measure and cut precise square pieces for patchwork.

RAFFIA A natural plant fibre derived from a species of palm. Artificial, brightly coloured versions are available from craft shops.

RICKRACK, BRAID A decorative zigzag woven braid used for trimming.

ROCAILLE BEADS Tiny glass seed beads, available in many colours, which are sewn down with a fine needle.

STRANDED EMBROIDERY THREAD A soft, loosely woven thread, which comes in six strands and which can be separated.

TACKING A large, temporary running stitch which is used to hold fabrics together before quilting or seaming, usually worked in a contrasting thread. This is taken out after the permanent stitches have been worked.

TAPESTRY FRAME An adjustable embroidery frame for supporting larger pieces of canvas or backing fabric.

TAPESTRY WOOL A twisted yarn used for working needlepoint.

TEMPLATE A pattern outline.

TENSION The number of stitches and rows to be worked per inch so that a finished knitted garment is the correct size.

TRAMÉ Laid threads worked on a double tapestry canvas.

TROMPE-L' OEIL A realistic image which has been designed to "deceive the eye".

WADDING A washable, polyester fibre, available by length, which is used as the padded filling layer in a quilt.

WARP THREAD The threads which run along the length of a woven fabric.

WATER-SOLUBLE FABRIC A plant-derived supporting fabric, used for machine embroidery, which dissolves in water.

WEAVER'S KNOT Also known as a reef knot, a strong flat knot used for joining two ends of thread.

WEFT THREAD The threads which run across the width of a woven fabric, from edge to edge.

Index